# Spiral Slide Rule: Equivalent to a Straight Slide Rule 83 Feet 4 Inches Long, Or, a Circular Rule 13 Feet 3 Inches in Diameter - Primary Source Edition

George Fuller

# SPIRAL SLIDE RULE.

EQUIVALENT TO

A STRAIGHT SLIDE RULE 83 FEET 4 INCHES LONG, OR, A CIRCULAR RULE 13 FEET 3 INCHES IN DIAMETER.

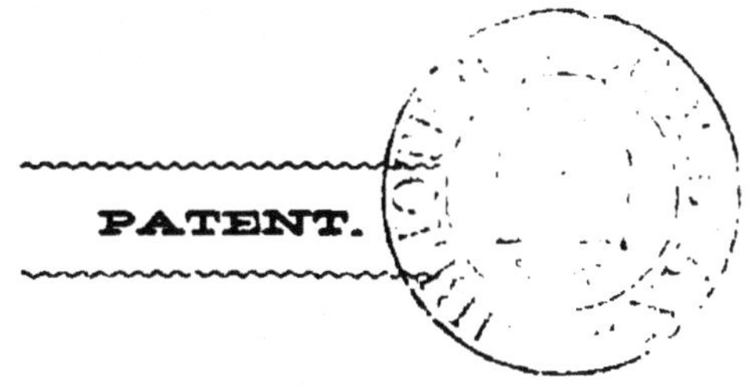


GEORGE FULLER, M. Inst. C.E.,

PROFESSOR OF ENGINEERING IN THE QUEEN'S UNIVERSITY, IRELAND.

LONDON:

E. & F. N. SPON, 46, CHARING CROSS.

New York: 446, BROOME STREET.

1878.

# SPIRAL SLIDE RULE.

The method of performing by mechanical means the work of addition and subtraction required when multiplying and dividing numbers by means of logarithms, originated with Gunter about the year 1606. He constructed a linear scale which was composed of two equal parts, and each half divided into parts proportional to the logarithms of numbers from 10 to 100. With this scale he used a pair of compasses for making the additions and subtractions.

About the year 1630, Oughtred invented the two similar logarithmic scales sliding in contact, which are at present in use; and he is stated to have used both straight and concentric circular scales. The advantage of this arrangement is, that the result is obtained by one motion of the sliding scale; and not only are multiplication and division thus worked, but questions in proportion, or the combination of the two, are solved by a single movement of the slide.

The simplicity of this method of calculating with figures is so great, that it seems strange it has not been more used; but the following considerations will, it is believed, account for this:—

In testing the relative advantages of different methods of making arithmetical calculations, the mental effort required, the time occupied, and the truth of the result have all to be taken into account. Now, in judging the ordinary slide rule by these points, it will be found that the facilities it offers are more apparent than real.

It is easy, with a little practice, to place one of the lines of the slide either opposite to a division of the rule or in a required position between two divisions, if these are not very close together. When the space, however, between two consecutive marks is very small, then great difficulty arises, from the strain upon the eyesight and the minute motion of the slide.

For example, in the ordinary slide rule with the scale $5\frac{1}{2}$ inches long, the breadth of the division from 99 to 100 is about $\frac{1}{40}$ of an inch. Therefore to mark such a number as 996, this space must be mentally divided into ten equal parts, each part consequently being $\frac{1}{400}$ of an inch, a magnitude quite inappreciable without a magnifying glass. The effort and time for the above is, however, slight, compared to that required when a point on one scale between two divisions has to be placed or read as agreeing with a point on the other, also between two divisions. For in this case (which is the most common, owing to the number of divisions on the ordinary slide rule necessarily being few) the division on one scale has to be mentally divided, and the particular point required fixed in the mind by its distance from the nearest division. Then the division on the other scale has to be mentally divided, and that part of it read which agrees with the point on the first scale previously fixed in the mind. Thus, for example, suppose it is required to place 554 on one scale to agree with 643 on the other. There are marks at 55 and 56 on one scale, and at 64 and 65 on the other; but the $\frac{4}{10}$ part of the distance between 55 and 56 has to be made to coincide with the $\frac{3}{10}$ part of that between 64 and 65: the difficulty not being to divide either of these distances into ten parts, if they are not very small, but to combine the two operations together.

If at the same time the spaces between the marks are very small, the difficulty is greatly increased by the strain upon the eyesight.

With regard to the truth of the result, Mr. Heather, in his 'Treatise on Mathematical Instruments,' writes in relation to the foot slide rule: "The solution in fact may be considered as obtained to within a two-hundredth part of the whole." Now this approximation, though close considering the length of scale of the instrument, and sufficient for some, is not near enough for very many of the calculations required by engineers and architects.

From the above it appears that a slide rule to

be thoroughly efficient, so that calculations may be made by it with ease and rapidity, and practically correct results obtained, the length of the logarithmic scale should be such that the space between any two consecutive numbers is large enough to be easily distinguished by the unaided eye; that the scale should be read by indices, and not as in the present rules; and that the number of divisions should be so great and distinctly marked, that the result to be obtained may be easily read and practically correct.

This combination, it is believed, is attained in the spiral slide rule.

The rule consists of a cylinder (*d*) that can be moved up and down upon, and turned round, an axis (*f*), which is held by a handle (*e*). Upon this cylinder is wound in a spiral a single logarithmic scale. Fixed to the handle is an index (*b*). Two other indices (*c*) and (*a*), whose distance apart is the axial length of the complete spiral, are fixed to the cylinder (*g*). This cylinder slides in (*f*) like a telescope tube, and thus enables the operator to place these indices in any required position relative to (*d*). Two stops (*o*) and (*p*) are so fixed that when they are brought in contact, the index (*b*) points to the commencement of the scale. (*n*) and (*m*) are two scales, the one on the piece carrying the movable indices, the other on the cylinder (*d*).

It will at once be seen that by this arrangement the length of the logarithmic scale can be

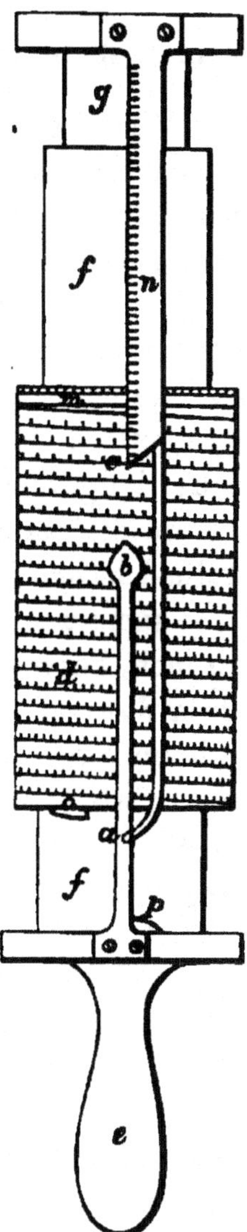


Scale, 3 inches to a foot.

made very great, whilst keeping the instrument of a convenient size for use. It requires only one logarithmic scale, so that every inch of the spiral scale is equivalent to two of the ordinary straight rule.

To fulfil with great exactness all the necessary conditions, the scale is made 500 inches, or 41 feet 8 inches, long—equivalent therefore to a straight rule 83 feet 4 inches long, and to a circular rule 13 feet 3 inches in diameter. This allows of results being obtained to one ten thousandth part of the whole, at the same time requiring no space less than $\frac{1}{48}$ of an inch, between any two consecutive numbers of four figures. The length of scale in the common rule only permits of the *first* figure of a number being printed; in this rule, the first *three* figures are printed throughout the scale. With this rule, to produce an error of one part in 200, there must be, either in setting or reading, an error of *one and one-tenth* inches. It will also be seen that both for setting and reading, indices are applied to the scale; so that these operations are performed with the greatest mental ease.

It may be remarked that the slide rule possesses an advantage over a table of logarithms, in addition to that of performing mechanically the requisite additions and subtractions, in that the approximation is uniform throughout the scale, and not nearer in one part than in another, as in the tables.

It must be remembered that all the calculations

founded on measurements of length, weight, and time, can only be approximative, as the data for them are so. Except therefore with the most refined measurements, it is a waste of time to carry results beyond the ten thousandth part of the whole.

## Rules.

In using the slide rule, the handle should be held in the left hand, the movable cylinder and indices being worked by the right, which holds the pen or pencil.

*Division of the Scale.*—Though this scale is large enough to admit of being read to four or even five figures, space does not allow of its being figured to more than three. Each of the primary divisions, as far as 650, is divided into ten parts, and from thence to 1000 into five parts; so that all numbers of four figures have either a mark upon the scale, or are midway between two marks. Thus 4786 is shown by a mark; also 8432; but 8431 is not shown by a mark, but is midway between 8430 and 8432. In a large part of the scale the space between these secondary divisions is large enough to be easily divided into parts by the eye. Thus many numbers of five figures are easily shown; for example, 26854. There are the first three figures at 268, then 5 is at the fifth secondary division, and the 4 must be estimated by the eye as $\frac{4}{10}$ of the space between 2685 and 2686. It must be noted that the same figures do not always mea same amount. Thus to represent 268540, 2685·4, 268·54, 26·854, 2·6854, ·26854, ·0 ·0026854, &c., the same point on the scale is

### MULTIPLICATION.

*Rule.*—Bring 100 to the fixed index, and the movable index to the multiplicand. move the cylinder so that the multiplier is fixed index. The quotient is read off at the movable indices.

*To ascertain the Value of the Quotient.*—Mo quently this may be determined by inspectio following rules will, however, give it in all ca

Consider a number like—

| | | | |
|---|---|---|---|
| 18763 | as one of | 5 | figures |
| 1876·3 | ,, | 4 | ,, |
| 187·63 | ,, | 3 | ,, |
| 18·763 | ,, | 2 | ,, |
| 1·8763 | ,, | 1 | ,, |
| ·18763 | ,, | 0 | ,, |
| ·018763 | ,, | −1 | ,, |
| ·0018763 | ,, | −2 | ,, |
| ·000187 | ,, | −3 | ,, |

Then the number of figures in the quot the algebraic sum of the number of figures multiplier and multiplicand, if it is *not* read the same index as the multiplicand. It is than that sum if read upon the same index.

*Examples.*—12 × ·142 = 1·704. The s

figures is two, and the answer is read from the same index as the multiplicand, so that the quotient has one figure.

64 × ·24 = 15·36. The sum of figures is two, but the answer is read at a different index to the multiplicand, and therefore the quotient has two figures.

12 × ·00142 = ·01704. The sum of the figure is 0, but the answer is read at the same index with the multiplicand, and therefore the quotient has one less, or minus one.

64 × ·0024 = ·1536. The sum of the figures is 0, and the answer is read at a different index to the multiplicand, and therefore the quotient has 0 figures.

48·42 × 64·34 = 3115·3. The sum of the figures is 4, and the answer is read at a different index to the multiplicand, and therefore the quotient has four figures.

## Division.

*Rule.*—Place *divisor* to fixed index, and the upper or lower movable index to the dividend, according as the first figure in the divisor is greater or less than the first figure in the dividend. Then move the cylinder so that the fixed index is at 100, and read the quotient at one of the movable indices.

The number of figures in the quotient is the algebraic *difference* between the number of figures in the dividend and divisor, if it is *not* read upon the same index as the dividend. It is one *more* than that difference if read upon the same index.

*Examples.*—$1468 \div 63 = 23 \cdot 3$, as the difference is 2, and the quotient is *not* read upon the same index as the dividend.

$1468 \div 125 = 11 \cdot 7$, as the difference is 1, and the quotient *is* read upon the same index as the dividend, and therefore has *two* figures.

$\cdot 1468 \div 63 = \cdot 00233$, as the difference is $-2$, and the quotient is *not* read upon the same index as the dividend, and therefore has $-2$ figures.

$1468 \div \cdot 00125 = 1174000$, as the difference is $4 - (-2) = 4 + 2 = 6$, and the quotient *is* read upon the same index as the dividend, and therefore has *seven* figures.

## MULTIPLICATION AND DIVISION.

*Rule.*—Move the cylinder so as to place the denominator to the fixed index. Then place movable index to one of the numerators. Then move the cylinder so that the fixed index points to the other numerator, and read the quotient at one of movable indices.

The number of figures in the quotient is the algebraic difference between the sum of the number of figures in the numerator and in the denominator, if it is read upon the *same* index as a factor of the numerator. It is *one more* than that difference if read upon the other index.

*Example.* $\frac{4854 \times 32 \cdot 6}{536} = 295 \cdot 22$, as the difference is $4 + 2 - 3 = 3$, and the quotient is read at the same index as either 4854 or 32·6 is placed.

$$\frac{\cdot 0764 \times \cdot 032}{14 \cdot 63} = \cdot 000167,$$ as the difference is $(-1) + (-1) - 2 = -4$, and the quotient is not read upon the index, that either ·0764 or ·032 is placed, and therefore *the number* of figures is $-3$.

To multiply three numbers together when one of them is a constant in frequent use.

*Rule.*—Find the *reciprocal* of the constant by division, and use it as the divisor in the preceding rule.

## Ratio.

When either of the movable indices is at one number and the fixed index at another, and the cylinder is turned into any other position, though the numbers at the indices will be different, their ratio will remain constant.

*Example.*—To convert francs and centimes into sterling money, supposing exchange 25f. 45c. for 1*l.* The ratio between centimes and pence is 2545 to 240. Place the cylinder so that the fixed index is at 2545, and make one of the movable indices point to 240. Then on moving the cylinder to read off different numbers of centimes at the fixed index, the corresponding value in pence will be read at the movable index.

*Wages Table.*—To find the wages for different times at 35*s.* per week of 57 hours. Place the

cylinder so that the fixed index is at 57, and make one of the movable indices point to 420, the number of pence in 35*s*. Then on moving the cylinder to read off different numbers of hours at the fixed index, the corresponding wages in pence will be read at the movable index.

## Proportion.

To find a third proportion to two numbers— $a : b :: b : c$

$c = \frac{b \times b}{a}$. Proceed according to rule for multiplication and division.

To find a fourth proportion to three numbers— $a : b :: c : d$

$d = \frac{b \times c}{a}$. Proceed according to rule for multiplication and division.

## Powers and Roots.

To obtain the square, cube, and fourth power of a number. The quickest way with this rule is by direct multiplication.

For higher powers and roots. Place the upper movable index ($c$) to the number, and read the scales ($n$ and $m$). These together give the *mantissa* of the logarithm of the number. To this the *index* has to be added. The index of the logarithm of a number greater than unity is *one less* than the number of figures in the integral part of that number. Thus the index of 5432 is 3, of 543·2 is 2, of 54·32 is 1, and of 5·432 is 0.

Multiply or divide the resulting number by the power or root, as shown above. Then place the cylinder so that it reads on the scales (*n* and *m*) the decimal part of the quotient. The power or root is then at the index (*c*). In the result the number of figures before the decimal point is *one more* than the number in the integral part of the above quotient.

The scale (*n*) is read from the *lowest line* of the top spiral and (*m*) from the vertical edge of the scale (*n*).

*Examples.*—$5^{13}$, on placing (*c*) to 500, scale (*n*) reads ·68 and scale (*m*) ·01897, which gives the logarithm of 5 – ·69897, the index being 0. Then ·69897 × 13 = 9·08661. Now placing the cylinder so that it reads ·08661 on scales (*n* and *m*) the index (*c*) reads 12207, and the required power is 1220700000, having 10 figures, as the integral part of the above quotient is 9.

$\sqrt[5]{741}$ on placing (*c*) to 741, scale (*n*) reads ·86 and scale (*m*) ·00982 which gives the logarithm of 741 – 2·86982, the index being 2. Then 2·86982 ÷ 5 = ·57396. Now placing the cylinder so that it reads ·57396 on scales (*n* and *m*) the index (*c*) reads 37495, and the required root is 3·7495, having one figure before the decimal point, as the integral part of the above quotient is 0.

## Powers of Decimal Fractions.

To avoid the use of negative indices, which often lead to erroneous results unless they are frequently used, the following method may be adopted :—

Write them as vulgar fractions, the numerator being expressed in units and decimals, and raise the numerator and denominator to the required power, the former by the method given above; the latter can be written down at once.

$$\text{Thus } \cdot 47^5 = \left(\frac{4\cdot 7}{10}\right)^5 \qquad \cdot 047^3 = \left(\frac{4\cdot 7}{100}\right)^3$$

### Roots of Decimal Fractions.

Write them as vulgar fractions, and multiply numerator and denominator by ten or a power of ten, so that the denominator may have a complete root. Then take the required root of the numerator by the method given above, and of the denominator by inspection :

$$\text{Thus } \sqrt{\cdot 4} = \sqrt{\frac{4}{10}} = \sqrt{\frac{40}{10^2}} = \frac{\sqrt{40}}{10}$$

$$\sqrt[3]{\cdot 04} = \sqrt[3]{\frac{4}{10^2}} = \sqrt[3]{\frac{40}{10^3}} = \frac{\sqrt[3]{40}}{10}$$

$$\sqrt[5]{\cdot 586} = \sqrt[5]{\frac{586}{10^3}} = \sqrt[5]{\frac{58600}{10^5}} = \frac{\sqrt[5]{58600}}{10}$$

$$\sqrt[3]{\cdot 00065} = \sqrt[3]{\frac{65}{10^5}} = \sqrt[3]{\frac{650}{10^6}} = \frac{\sqrt[3]{650}}{10^2}$$

$$(\cdot 0434)^{\frac{5}{6}} = \left(\frac{434}{10^4}\right)^{\frac{5}{6}} = \left(\frac{43400}{10^6}\right)^{\frac{5}{6}} = \frac{(43400)^{\frac{5}{6}}}{10^5}$$

### SIMPLE INTEREST.

Let P be the Principal in pounds and parts of a pound;

$n$ the number of years and parts of a year for which interest is taken;

$r$ the interest of one pound for one year;

M the amount.

$M = P + P n r.$

Also P is the present value of M, due at the end of the time $n$.

$$P = \frac{M}{1 + n r}.$$

In practice the *discount* is the interest of the sum of money paid before it is due;

$$\text{or } D = M n r.$$

### COMPOUND INTEREST.

Let P be the Principal in pounds and parts of a pound;

$n$ number of years for which interest is taken;

$r$ the interest of one pound for one year;

M the amount.

Interest due once a year.

$$M = P(1 + r)^n \qquad n = \frac{\log. M - \log. P}{\log. (1 + r)}$$

Let interest be due $q$ times a year and $\frac{r}{q}$ the interest of one pound for $\frac{1}{q}$ part of a year,

$$M = P\left(1 + \frac{r}{q}\right)^{q n}.$$

VALUE OF r.

| Per Cent. | | Per Cent. | | Per Cent. | | Per Cent. | | Per Cent. | |
|---|---|---|---|---|---|---|---|---|---|
| $\frac{1}{16}$ | ·000625 | $\frac{3}{8}$ | ·00375 | $\frac{11}{16}$ | ·006875 | 1 | ·01 | 6 | ·0( |
| $\frac{1}{8}$ | ·00125 | $\frac{7}{16}$ | ·004375 | $\frac{3}{4}$ | ·0075 | 2 | ·02 | 7 | ·0 |
| $\frac{3}{16}$ | ·001875 | $\frac{1}{2}$ | ·005 | $\frac{13}{16}$ | ·008125 | 3 | ·03 | 8 | ·0 |
| $\frac{1}{4}$ | ·0025 | $\frac{9}{16}$ | ·005625 | $\frac{7}{8}$ | ·00875 | 4 | ·04 | 9 | ·( |
| $\frac{5}{16}$ | ·003125 | $\frac{5}{8}$ | ·00625 | $\frac{15}{16}$ | ·009375 | 5 | ·05 | 10 | · |

The tables printed on the rule have been mac and selected as those considered most usefı Owing to our want of a decimal system, it l been deemed most important to have a serie of tables which give for our measures of weigh length, time, &c., the equivalent decimal fract of the larger for successive numbers of tl smaller unit. This enables results to be obtain without the necessity of reduction. Thus to fir the area of a rectangle whose sides are 24′ 6 and 43′ 5½″. The table gives by inspect ·5208 and ·4583 opposite 6¼″ and 5½″ resp tively, so that the area is obtained by multiplyi 24·521 by 43·458. The result, as shown by t rule, is 1065·6. If the parts of a square f are required in twelfths, the table shows th ·6 of a foot is equivalent to 7¼ twelfths, and tl result reads 1065 – 7¼.

LONDON: PRINTED BY WILLIAM CLOWES AND SONS, STAMFORD STREI AND CHARING CROSS.

CPSIA information can be obtained
at www.ICGtesting.com
Printed in the USA
LVOW03s1338250816
501847LV00016B/347/P

9 781293 8054

# Supplement To Danas Mineralogy: First Supplement To Dana's Minerology, Volume 1...

James Dwight Dana

**Aphrosiderite**, *a Chlorite-like mineral* [p. 297].—Analysis by v. Hauer (Jahrb. geol. Reichs., 1854, 79, and J. f. pr. Chem., lxiii, 30):

$\dddot{Si}$ 26·08 $\ddot{\overline{Al}}$ 20·27 $\dot{Fe}$ 32·91 $\dot{Mg}$ 10·00 $\dot{H}$ 10·06 = 99·32

affording the oxygen ratio for the protoxyds, peroxyds, silica and water, 5:4·17:5·97:3·95, or quite nearly 5:4:6:4. Von Hauer appears to prefer the ratio 5:3:6:4 and deduces the formula $\ddot{Al}\,\dot{H}^4+\dot{R}^5\,\dddot{Si}^2$, and remarks on the nearness of the formula to that of chlorite (Rose), as written by Kenngott.

The aphrosiderite occurs in calcite and specular iron in minute, lustrous, crystalline laminæ, of a deep olive-green color. Rather easily decomposed by muriatic acid.

[Taking the ratio 5:4:6:4 which the analysis gives, the oxygen ratio between all the bases and the silica (excluding the water) is then 9:6 = 3:2, the same as in ripidolite (Rose), which would give the ripidolite formula $(\dot{R}^3, \ddot{\overline{Al}})\,\dddot{Si}^{\frac{3}{2}}+Aq$ in which $\dot{R}^3$ and $\ddot{\overline{Al}}$ are here to one another as 4:5; or including these proportions $(\frac{4}{9}\dot{R}^3+\frac{5}{9}\ddot{\overline{Al}})\,\dddot{Si}^{\frac{3}{2}}+Aq$.

The ratio adopted by von Hauer, 5:3:6:4, gives for the oxygen ratio of the bases and silica 8:6 = 4:3, which is the ratio of chlorite (Rose). Thus the liberty taken with the analysis in deducing the ratios is sufficient to transfer the mineral from one of these species to the other.—D.]

ARSENOMELAN and SCLEROCLASE, *von Waltershausen.*—Description and analysis by W. S. von Waltershausen (Pogg., xciv, 123):—Occurs with the Dufrenoysite in the Binnen Valley in dolomite. Form trimetric: a brachydome of 115° 16′; angle between a plane of the brachydome and that of a macrodome 134° 59′; axes *a* (vertical axis): *b*:*c* = 0·6538:1:1·0815, [giving for the fundamental vertical prism 91° 47′]. Crystals longitudinally striated. Color lead-gray to tin-white, also steel-gray to iron black. Analyses:

| | | S | As | Pb | Ag | Fe | |
|---|---|---|---|---|---|---|---|
| I. Lead gray; | G. = 5·393 | 25·910 | 28·556 | 44·564 | 0·424 | 0·448 | = 99·922 |
| II. | G. = 5·405 | 24·658 | 25·740 | 47·586 | 0·938 | —— | = 98·922 |
| III. | G. = 5·469 | 23·949 | 26·458 | 49·657 | 0·629 | —— | = 100·693 |

Atomic ratio for the bases, arsenic and sulphur in I, 0·36:0·61:1·29; in II, 0·38:0·555:1·24; in III, 0·38:0·56:1·185. As the ratios do not correspond to a simple formula, von Waltershausen regards the compound as consisting of two *isomorphous* compounds, $PbS+As^2S^3$ (A) and $2PbS+As^2S^3$ (B), and calculates that I, contains A and B in the ratio 3·124:1; II, in the ratio 1:1·234; III, in the ratio 1:0·966. He gives the name *Arsenomelan* to A, and *Scleroclase* to B. He observes that A is the formula of zinkenite, except that it contains arsenic in place of antimony, while Scleroclase (B) differs only in its arsenic from heteromorphite or feather ore. The composition of scleroclase is near that obtained by Damour in his analysis of dufrenoysite [see Min., p. 77].

[Zinkenite and Heteromophite are both regarded as trimetric; yet as far as is known, they are far from homœomorphous: for zinkenite has a prism of 120° and occurs in *hexagonal* compound crystals, while heteromorphite is not in such twins and according to von Waltershausen has nearly the form above given for arsenomelan. The hypothesis that A and B are isomorphous appears therefore to need evidence to sustain it. The angles of arsenomelan are near those of bournonite.—D.]

**Atacamite** [p. 138].—Analysis of the atacamite of Copiapo, Chili, by F. Field, (Q. J. Chem. Soc., vii, 193):

| | | | | | | | |
|---|---|---|---|---|---|---|---|
| 1. | Cl 14·94 | Cu 56·46 | $\dot{H}$ 17·79 | = | Cu Cl 28·22 | $\dot{Cu}$ 53·99 | $\dot{H}$ 17·79 |
| 2. | 15·01 | 56·24 | 18·00 | = | 28·35 | 53·62 | 18·00 |

whence the formula Cu Cl + 3Cu O + 5H O. Specific gravity 4·25.

Mallet obtained in an analysis of atacamite (Ramm., 5th Suppl., 57), $\dot{Cu}$ 55·94, Cu 14·54, Cl 16·33, $\dot{H}$ 12·96, Quartz 0·08 = 99·85.

**Automolite** [p. 103].—Occurs at Bridgewater, Vermont.

**Baltimorite** [p. 282].—In the Jahrbuch geol. Reichsanstalt, Wien, 1853, No. 1, p. 154, C. von Hauer published an analysis of a specimen from Texas, Pa., labelled Baltimorite, which is copied in the Mineralogy, p. 285, making it to contain 27·15 of silica, 26 of magnesia, &c. In Kenngott's Min. Notizen, No. 11, a very different result by von Hauer is published apparently from the same investigation. The specimen was a fibrous, grayish or reddish gray mineral, affording 60·53 p. c. soluble in acids, (15 p. c. of this carbonic acid, and 8·86 of water,) 39·85 p. c. insoluble in acids. From such a mixture, after a series of estimates, Baltimorite is judged to have a composition corresponding to the percentage :

| $\dddot{\text{Si}}$ | $\bar{\text{Al}}$ | $\dot{\text{Fe}}$ | $\dot{\text{Ca}}$ | $\dot{\text{Mg}}$ | $\dot{\text{H}}$ |
|---|---|---|---|---|---|
| 25·88 | 13·00 | 7·33 | 14·29 | 21·11 | 18·41 |

for which the formula given is $[\dot{\text{H}}^{3}\,\bar{\text{Al}}+\dot{\text{R}}\,\dddot{\text{Si}}]+[4(\dot{\text{Mg}}\,\dot{\text{Ca}}+\dot{\text{H}})+(\dot{\text{Mg}},\dot{\text{Ca}})\,\dddot{\text{Si}}]$

[Thus we have a new analysis of a stone which somebody has labelled Baltimorite. It is very wide from the original Baltimorite of Thomson (from Bare Hills, Maryland); and is no better entitled to the name than many other fibrous stones that could be gathered from our serpentine regions. Taken as an analysis of a mineral from a serpentine region, it can hardly be esteemed of much value on account of the mixtures with it; as a correction of former accounts of the mineral Baltimorite, it is only perplexing the subject.]

Barnhardite [p. 500].—Dr. F. A. Genth, Am. J. Sci., xix, 17.

Barytocelestine [p. 369].—Analysis by von Waltershausen of a heavy spar containing sulphate of strontia from the dolomite of Binnen Valley in the Alps (Pogg., xciv, 134) :—$\dot{\text{Ba}}\,\dddot{\text{S}}$ 87·792, $\dot{\text{Sr}}\,\dddot{\text{S}}$ 9·070, $\dddot{\text{Si}}$ 0·685, $\bar{\text{Al}}$ 2·155=99·702. It occurs in nests or druses of crystals.

Baulite [p. 248].—A specimen of this mineral consisting of an aggregation of quite small glassy crystals or grains resembling glassy feldspar in appearance, has been received by the writer from Dr. F. A. Genth. Under the suspicion that the excess of silica in the analysis might be due to mixed quartz, I examined it with a microscope, but could not satisfy myself that there was any quartz present. It appeared to be purely the baulite. The published analysis by Genth (Ann. Chem. Pharm., lxvi, 270), and Forchhammer (Skand. Nat. Samm., i, Stockholm), make the species a feldspar, in which the oxygen ratio for the protoxyds, peroxyds and silica, according to the former, is 1 : 3 : 24.—d.

Beckite, Duf. Min., iii, 750.—A siliceous coral from Devonshire according to Kenngott, Ber. Wien Acad., x, 292.

Biotite [p. 225].—Analysis of the mica of Greenwood Furnace, by C. v. Hauer (Kenngott Min. Not., No. 12). Mean of results :

| $\dddot{\text{Si}}$ | $\bar{\text{Al}}$ | $\bar{\text{Fe}}$ | $\dot{\text{Ca}}$ | $\dot{\text{Mg}}$ | $\dot{\text{K}}$ | $\dot{\text{Na}}$ | ign. |
|---|---|---|---|---|---|---|---|
| 40·21 | 19·99 | 7·96 | 1·55 | 21·15 | 5·22 | 0·90 | 2·89 = 98·97 |

Oxygen ratio for $\dot{\text{R}}$, $\bar{\text{R}}$, $\dddot{\text{Si}}$, 1 : 1·18 : 2·13 or 1 : 1 : 2, as in most biotites. The paper contains a review of the analyses of biotite.

[Smith and Brush obtained for the oxygen ratio from their analyses of this biotite 11·26 : 9·38 : 20·63. The sum of the oxygen of the bases equals 20·64, or just the oxygen of the silica; and the same holds true in v. Hauer's analysis, each corresponding to the general formula ($\dot{\text{R}}^{3}$, $\bar{\text{R}}$) $\dddot{\text{Si}}$.—d.] See further, *Phlogopite*.

Bismuthine [p. 33, 503].—Occurrence of bismuthine in Rowan Co., North Carolina, F. A. Genth, Am. J. Sci., [2], xix, 16.

Bohnerz [p. 131].—R. Schenck (Ann. d. Ch. u. Pharm., xc, 123, and J. f. pr. Ch., lxii, 313) shows by analysis that the bohnerz of Kandern is a clayey or argillaceous limonite.

Boltonite [p. 167].—Boltonite, according to analyses by Dr. J. Lawrence Smith, is identical with chrysolite. He obtained (Amer. J. Sci., [2], xviii, 372,) as a mean of his results :

$\dddot{\text{Si}}$ 42·31 $\dot{\text{Mn}}$ 51·16 $\dot{\text{Fe}}$ 2·78 $\bar{\text{Al}}$ 0·17 loss by heat 1·90

Analysis of boltonite by v. Hauer (Kenngott's Min. Not., No. 12):

$\dddot{\text{Si}}$ 13·32 $\dot{\text{Fe}}$ 3·80 $\dot{\text{Ca}}$ 29·00 $\dot{\text{Mg}}$ 21·17 $\ddot{\text{C}}$ (by loss) 32·71 = 100

The boltonite was analyzed mixed with the carbonates in which it was imbedded, amounting to about ⅔ds the portion employed.

[The results of von Hauer differ widely from these of Dr. Smith, and as we have independent testimony to the general correctness of Dr. Smith's analyses, in analyses by another not yet completed, von Hauer's must be erroneous. The method adopted by von Hauer allows of too many uncertainties to be free from doubt.—D.]

Boracic Compounds [p. 392].—On the Boracic compounds of the Tuscan Lagoons, E. Bechi, Am. J. Sci., [2], xix, 119.

Brevicite [p. 327], from Clinkstone near Oberschaffhausen in Kaiserstuhl.—E. Tobler obtained in an analysis (Ann. Ch. u. Pharm., xci, 229):

| $\ddot{Si}$ | $\ddot{\overline{Al}}$ | $\dot{Ca}$ | $\dot{Mg}$ | $\dot{Na}$ | $\dot{K}$ | $\dot{H}$ | |
|---|---|---|---|---|---|---|---|
| 43·085 | 29·214 | 12·551 | 0·714 | 3·152 | 0·398 | 11·000 | = 100·114 |

corresponding to $\dot{R}^3 \ddot{Si}^2 + 3\ddot{\overline{Al}} \ddot{Si} + 6\dot{H}$. The oxygen ratio afforded by the analysis for $\dot{R}$, $\ddot{\overline{R}}$, $\ddot{Si}$ and $\dot{H}$ is, 1 : 3·09 : 5·18 : 2·22. Specific gravity 2·246; hardness = 6; when pulverized gelatinizes in muriatic acid.

Brongniardite.—Occurs in combinations of the regular octahedron and dodecahedron: L. Sæmann. (Communicated.)

Brucite [p. 133].—Add to the locality in the Mineralogy: occurs in Texas, Pennsylvania. The crystal figured on p. 133 was from Low's Mine in Texas and not from Hoboken.

Cacoxene [p. 424].—Analysis by von Hauer (Jahrb. geol. Reichs., 1854, 73):

| $\overline{\dot{P}}$ | $\ddot{\overline{Fe}}$ | $\dot{Ca}$ | $\dot{H}$ (loss by ignition) | Insol. in mur. acid. | |
|---|---|---|---|---|---|
| 18·56 | 45·05 | *trace* | 30·94 | 3·63 | = 98·18 |

Excluding the insoluble portion, von Hauer's, Steinmann's and Richardson's results are as follows:

| | $\overline{\dot{P}}$ | $\ddot{\overline{Fe}}$ | $\dot{H}$ | |
|---|---|---|---|---|
| 1. | 19·63 | 47·64 | 32·72, | *von Hauer.* |
| 2. | 22·28 | 45·32 | 32·38, | *Steinmann.* |
| 3. | 21·85 | 45·94 | 32·19, | *Richardson.* |

giving alike the formula $\ddot{\overline{Fe}}^2 \overline{\dot{P}} + 12\dot{H}$ = phosphoric acid 21·17, sesquioxyd of iron 47·07, water 31·76=100.

Calcite [p. 435, 503.]—Analyses of different limestones of the Tyrol, by A. von Hubert, Jahrb. der geol. Reichs., i, 729, and J. f. pr. Chem., lxii, 225, 1854. Also analyses of limestone and dolomite from the Saltzburg Alps, by v. Lipold, J. f. pr. Chem., lxii, 228.

A peculiar earthy calcareous rock from the tufa of Pico Crux, Madeira, afforded E. Schweizer (J. f. pr. Chem. lxiii, 201), a large proportion of silica in the soluble state. The following were the results of the analysis:

| $\ddot{Si}$ | $\dot{Mg}$ | $\dot{Mg}\ddot{C}$ | $\dot{Ca}\ddot{C}$ | $\ddot{\overline{Fe}}$, $\overline{\dot{P}}$, etc. | Organ. subst. | $\dot{H}$ | Sand | |
|---|---|---|---|---|---|---|---|---|
| 20·88 | 5·39 | 5·15 | 52·12 | 0·36 | 4·76 | 10·00 | 1·57 | = 99·73 |

The 5·39 p. c. of magnesia are regarded as in combination with silica.

The limestone of Caniçal, Madeira, which is a modern formation of calcareous sands containing shells mainly of existing species, according to the same analyst, consists of

$\dot{Ca}\ddot{C}$ 84·29, $\dot{Mg}\ddot{C}$ 5·48, Phosphates 1·00, nitrog. org. subst. 4·66, $\dot{H}$ 2·41, Sand 1·48=99·32

Carpholite [p. 316].—Analysis by v. Hauer (Kenngott's Min. Not., No. 12):

| $\ddot{Si}$ | $\ddot{\overline{Al}}$ | $\ddot{\overline{Fe}}$ | $\ddot{\overline{Mn}}$ | $\dot{Ca}$ | Fl | $\dot{H}$ | |
|---|---|---|---|---|---|---|---|
| 36·15 | 19·74 | 9·87 | 20·76 | 1·83 | 1·74 | 10·19 | = 100·28 |

corresponding to $\ddot{\overline{R}} \ddot{Si} + 1\frac{1}{2}\dot{H}$. Crystallization trimetric; in groups of acicular crystals. [The oxygen ratio 1 : 1 : $\frac{1}{2}$ is identical with that of calamine.—D.]

Chalilite [p. 326].—A massive mineral associated with chalilite (see p. 326 of Min.), looking something like bole, afforded von Hauer (Kenngott's Min. Notiz., No. 11):

| $\ddot{Si}$ | $\ddot{\overline{Al}}$ | $\dot{Fe}$ | $\dot{Ca}$ | $\dot{Mg}$ | Mn | $\dot{K}$ | ign. | |
|---|---|---|---|---|---|---|---|---|
| 44·11 | 10·90 | 1·05 | 6·74 | 13·01 | *trace* | *trace* | 24·07 | = 99·88 |

The oxygen ratio for the protoxyds, peroxyds, silica and water, as deduced is, 9·204 : 6·863 : 29·211 : 26·744. Von Hauer adopts the ratio 4 : 3 : 12 : 13. [$4\frac{1}{2}$ : 3 : $13\frac{1}{2}$ : 12 is much nearer the analysis, but neither this nor the other leads to any formula.]

Chiolite [p. 98].—Imperfect crystals of chiolite, from the Topaz mine of Mursinsk in the Ural, have been measured by Kenngott (Sitzungsber., xi, 980). The form, according to his observations is trimetric, with the prismatic angle 124° 22′; the acute edge of the prism is truncated, giving the angle on the prismatic faces 117° 49′. These results are wide from those of Kokscharov, who describes the form as dimetric.

CHLOROPAL or UNGHWARITE [p. 504].—The analysis on p. 504 of Min. is a mean of two analyses. The result affords the oxygen ratio for the protoxyds, silica and water 1 : 6 : 3½. In the analyses of Brandes and Biewend, Kenngott supposes the iron may have been protoxyd instead of peroxyd (the latter the result of these chemists) and obtains thus the oxygen ratio 1 : 3 : 2.

CHLOROPHYLLITE [p. 215].—Measurements of a crystal of chlorophyllite are given by Kenngott (Min. Not., No. 11), and the conclusion arrived at, from the angles, that it was originally iolite, a fact which the unaltered iolite often associated with it places beyond doubt.

CHRYSOLITE [p. 184].—Observations on chrysolite by Dr. Scheerer, Handw. Chem. Lieb. Pogg., &c., 1853.

A slag from an Iron Furnace at Easton, Pa., afforded Dr. C. T. Jackson (Proc. Am. Assoc., iv, 384):

| $\dddot{\mathrm{Si}}$ | $\dot{\mathrm{Ca}}$ | $\dot{\mathrm{Fe}}$ | $\dot{\mathrm{Mn}}\,\dddot{\overline{\mathrm{Mn}}}$ | $\dddot{\overline{\mathrm{Al}}}$ |
|---|---|---|---|---|
| 35·70 | 31·80 | 18·00 | 14·90 | 3·50 = 101·90 |

Dr. Jackson observes that the iron and manganese were probably all protoxyd, and this gives the formula $(\dot{\mathrm{Ca}}, \dot{\mathrm{Fe}}, \dot{\mathrm{Mn}})^3\,\dddot{\mathrm{Si}}$. The crystals have a clove-brown color like axinite and are described as rhombohedral. [The formula is that of chrysolite. Crystals of this color and *probably* the same, from Easton, received by the writer from Dr. E. Swift, are rhombic prisms of 98° 48′, with the obtuse edge truncated and a macrodome of 132° 40′. The first angle corresponds to the prism 1ĭ in chrysolite which equals 99° 6′, and the last approaches i2̆, which equals 130° 2′.—D.]

CHRYSOTIL [p. 282].—Analysis of chrysotil from serpentine at Abbottsville, N. J., by E. L. Reakirt, under the direction of Dr. Genth, Amer. J. Sci., [2], xviii, 410.

CLINOCHLORE [p. 293].—M. N. de Kokscharov has measured anew the chlorite (ripidolite, von Kobell) of Achmatowsk, and come to the conclusion that the form is monoclinic, and that the species is identical with clinochlore which last name he adopts for it. No optical characters are given. Akad. Wiss. St. Petersburg, 1854, and Am. J. Sci., [2], xix, 176.

CLINTONITE [p. 297, 505].—Analyses by Plattner (Breith. Min., ii, 385) of a specimen from Amity:

| $\dddot{\mathrm{Si}}$ | $\dddot{\overline{\mathrm{Al}}}$ | $\dddot{\overline{\mathrm{Fe}}}$ | $\dot{\mathrm{Mg}}$ | $\dot{\mathrm{Ca}}$ | $\dot{\mathrm{H}}$ |
|---|---|---|---|---|---|
| 21·4 | 46·7 | 4·3 | 9·8 | 12·5 | 3·5 = 98·2 |

The zirconia in the analysis, p. 505 of Min. was due to zircon mechanically mixed.

COPIAPITE [p. 387].—Dr. J. L. Smith obtained in his analyses the formula $\dddot{\overline{\mathrm{Fe}}}\,\dddot{\mathrm{S}}^2 + 11\dot{\mathrm{H}}$. G. = 1·84. Amer. J. Sci., [2], xviii, 375.

COUZERANITE [p. 206].—In part altered scapolite according to Kenngott, Sitzungsber., xii, 714. One specimen examined was different, but composition not ascertained; form a square or perhaps rhombic prism. H. = 6·5. G. = 2·85.

CUBAN [p. 68].—Analysis by Dr. J. Lawrence Smith, agreeing with Prof. Booth's, Am. J. Sci., [2], xviii, 381.

DANBURITE [p. 212].—Specific gravity by a new determination, 2·958, G. J. Brush.

DATHOLITE [p. 334].—The crystalline form of the datholite of Andreasberg has been studied by R. Hess (Pogg. Ann., xciii, 380). He obtained for the inclination of *O* on *i*ĭ 89° 56·2′ in one crystal, and 89° 59·2′ in another; and from these and his other measurements concludes that the axis is vertical, or at least within 1 minute of 90°. He obtained for *I* : *I* (see Min. for lettering, and this Jour., xvii, 215) 115° 15·2′; for i2̆ : i2̆ = 76° 42′; 2ĭ : 2ĭ (over *O*) = 115° 25′. [The datholite of Roaring Brook afforded the writer for *I* : *I*, 115° 12′.—D.]

Analysis of crystals from the Gabro Rosso, Mt. Caporciano, Tuscany, by Bechi, (Am. J. Sci., [2], xiv, 65):

$\dddot{\mathrm{Si}}$ 37·500 $\dddot{\overline{\mathrm{Al}}}$ 0·852 $\dot{\mathrm{Ca}}$ 35·341 $\dot{\mathrm{Mg}}$ 2·121 $\dddot{\mathrm{B}}$ 22·083 $\dot{\mathrm{H}}$ 1·562 = 99·413

whence Bechi deduces the formula $2(\dot{\mathrm{Ca}}^3\,\dddot{\mathrm{Si}}^4 + 3\dot{\mathrm{Ca}}\,\dddot{\mathrm{B}}) + \dot{\mathrm{Mg}}\,\dot{\mathrm{H}}^2$ = $\dddot{\mathrm{Si}}$ 38·75, $\dddot{\mathrm{B}}$ 21·93, $\dot{\mathrm{Ca}}$ 35·36, $\dot{\mathrm{Mg}}$ 2·09, $\dot{\mathrm{H}}$ 1·87. The small proportion of water is a remarkable peculiarity of this variety. [The ratio between the oxygen of the silica and all the other ingredients in this formula is 24 : 33, and in the analysis 24 : 34, or very nearly 2 : 3, which is probably the true ratio, affording the general formula $(\dot{\mathrm{R}}^3, \dot{\mathrm{H}}^3, \dddot{\mathrm{B}})\,\dddot{\mathrm{Si}}^{\frac{4}{3}}$].

Delvauxite [p. 427].—Analysis by von Hauer (Jahrb. k. k. geol. Reichs., 1854, 68, and J. f. pr. Ch. lxiii, 18), taking the percentage after excluding the silica:

| $\dddot{P}$ | $\ddot{F}e$ | $\dot{C}a$ | $\dot{H}$ |
|---|---|---|---|
| 20·93 | 52·03 | 7·94 | 19·08 = 99·98 |
| 20·04 | 52·54 | 8·37 | 19·04 = 99·99 |

Von Hauer thence deduces the formula $\dot{C}a^3\dddot{P} + \ddot{F}e^5\dddot{P} + 16\dot{H}$.

Diamond [p. 24].—A large diamond of pure water, from the Province of Minas Geraes, Brazil, has been described by Dufrenoy. It is a dodecahedron with bevelled edges, and weighs 254½ carats. It is called the "Star of the South." There are impressions of diamond crystals in it, showing that it is one of a cluster that were formed together probably in a geode like quartz crystals. L'Institut, No. 1096, and Am. J. Sci., [2], xix, 288.

Diaspore [p. 128].—The locality of diaspore at the Topaz vein, Trumbull, Conn., mentioned on page 483 of Min., may be added at page 129.

Dolomite [p. 441].—Analysis and description of the dolomite of the Binnen Valley, in the Alps, containing the Dufrenoysite, &c., by W. S. v. Waltershausen (Pogg., xcii, 115): Structure saccharoidal; G.=2·845. Composition, $\ddot{C}$ 45·566, $\dot{C}a$ 29·852, $\dot{M}g$ 20·488, insoluble 3·314=99·220, or very nearly 1 of $\dot{C}a\ddot{C}$ to 1 of $\dot{M}g\ddot{C}$. Besides Dufrenoysite, the dolomite contains blende, pyrites, orpiment, realgar, arsenomelan, etc.

Dufrenoysite [p. 77].—Analysis of Dufrenoysite by W. S. v. Waltershausen (Pogg., xciv, 120):

| S | As | Ag | Pb | Cu | Fe |
|---|---|---|---|---|---|
| 27·546 | 30·059 | 1·229 | 2·749 | 37·746 | 0·824 = 100·153 |

affording von Waltershausen the formula, the iron being supposed to be in the condition of mixed pyrites, $[R^3S + As^2S^3] + RS$ in which R is mainly copper.

Von Waltershausen says that in Damour's analysis the mineral used must have been mixed with arsenomelan (q. v.). He was careful to analyse the monometric crystals. G. =4·477, mean of 3 determinations.

Edingtonite [p. 323].—Analysis by M. F. Heddle (Phil. Mag., [4], ix, 179), $\dddot{S}i$ 36·98, $\ddot{A}l$ 22·63, $\dot{B}a$ 26·84, $\dot{C}a$ and $\dot{N}a$ *trace*, $\dot{H}$ 12·46=98·91. G. =2·694. The analysis, p. 323, is the deduced percentage corresponding to the formula.—*Glottalite* of Thomson is regarded by Mr. Heddle as impure Edingtonite.

Ehlite [p. 426].—According to Kenngott (Sitzungsber, xii, 26), the Ehlite from Ehl near Linz on the Rhine, is similar in form to liroconite, being trimetric; the summit is a dome, or two planes meeting in an edge.

Eukolite [p. 343].—Trimetric, with an angle of 120° nearly, having 3 cleavages, meeting at an angle of 60°; and a fourth at right angles with the three; optically biaxial according to Damour: L. Sæmann. (Communicated.)

Euxenite [p. 358].—Description and analysis by David Forbes (Edinb. N. Phil. J., [2], i, 62). Mineral from Alve on Tromoen, an island near Arendal, Norway. Apparently trimetric; observed planes $\infty$, $\infty\text{-}\bar{\infty}$, $\infty\text{-}\breve{\infty}$, $m\text{-}\breve{\infty}$, 1. Approximate measurements by M. Dahl: $\infty : \infty\text{-}\breve{\infty} = 117°$, $\infty : \infty = 126°$, $\infty\text{-}\breve{\infty} : m\text{-}\breve{\infty} = 154° 30'$, $\infty\text{-}\breve{\infty} : 1 = 107°$. Cleavage none. H. =6·5; G. =4·99 at 60° F. of a small crystal; of a pure fragment of a crystal 4·89. Lustre brilliant and metallic vitreous; in very thin splinters translucent with a reddish brown color. Fracture conchoidal.

In a glass tube no change of color or lustre, B.B.; alone, infusible and unchanged; with borax in the oxydating flame, gives a brownish-yellow glass, somewhat lighter in color when cold; in the reducing flame unchanged, even on flaming; with salt of phosphorus, a glass greenish-yellow while hot, nearly colorless on cooling. No action of titanium or manganese although containing both of these metals. Composition:

| | $\ddot{C}b$ | $\ddot{T}i$ | $\ddot{A}l$ | $\dot{C}a$ | $\dot{M}g$ | $\dot{Y}$ | $\dot{C}e$ | $\dot{F}e$ | $\ddot{U}$ | $\dot{H}$ |
|---|---|---|---|---|---|---|---|---|---|---|
| | 38·58 | 14·36 | 3·12 | 1·27 | 0·19 | 29·36 | 3·31 | 1·98 | 5·22 | 2·88 = 100·37 |
| Oxygen | 4·53 | 5·79 | 1·45 | 0·38 | 0·07 | 5·87 | 0·47 | 0·43 | 0·61 | 2·56 |

Some columbic acid is mixed with the titanic acid. The oxygen in the columbic acid (Rose's niobic) is deduced from the atomic weight of tantalum. The ratio for the acids and bases, excluding the water is 10·32 : 9·28.

[If the titanic acid be reckoned with the bases (see Min.) the ratio is 4·53 : 15·07, which, allowing for some columbic acid with the titanic acid, may point to the ratio 1 : 3; this would give the formula $\dot{\text{R}}\,\ddot{\text{C}}\text{b}$ or $(\overline{\text{R}}, \dot{\text{R}}^3)\,\ddot{\text{C}}\text{b}^3$, which is analogous to the formula of tantalite. There is some approximation to the form of tantalite, the occurring prism being 126° in euxenite, and 122° 54′ in tantalite; or, taking another view of their relative positions, the angle 117° above may correspond to $O : \frac{3}{2}\breve{\imath}$ in tantalite which is 117° 2′. But without further crystallographic examinations it would be premature to assert a near relation.—D.]

**Feldspars** [p. 228].—A review of the various analyses of different species of the feldspar and scapolite families of minerals is given by Scheerer in the Handwörterbuch d. Chemie, Braunschw., 1853, and an abstract, in Neues Jahrb., 1854, 593.

**Felsobanyite** [p. 134].—Felsobanyite of Haidinger has been referred to gibbsite. Haidinger sustains it as a good species in the Sitzungsber., xii, 183. giving the following characters. Usually in concretions; also in 6-sided folia, with two angles of 112°. Crystallization trimetric, optically biaxial. H.=1·5; G.=2·33 (Kenngott). Cleavage-face pearly. Color snow-white, surface often yellowish. Composition according to C. v. Hauer, $\overline{\text{Al}}^2\,\dddot{\text{S}} + 10\dot{\text{H}}$ = sulphuric acid 17·18, alumina 44·15, water 38·66. Analysis afforded:

| $\dddot{\text{S}}$ | $\overline{\text{Al}}$ | $\dot{\text{H}}$ | |
|---|---|---|---|
| 16·47 | 45·53 | 37·27 | = 99·27 |

The mineral is hence near websterite, and particularly paraluminite, [p. 509].

**Ficinite.**—*Ficinite* of Bernhardi, by some referred to Vivianite, has been examined by Kenngott (Min. Not., No. 11), and is described as follows: it is from Bodenmais in Bavaria, where it occurs with garnet, iolite, etc. Form monoclinic; cleavage perfect in one direction, and also in a second inclined 129° to the former, both parallel to the orthodiagonal. Color black; within greenish-brown. Lustre weak; waxy or pearly. Subtranslucent. H.=5.0–5·5; G.=3·4–3·53. In a glass tube yields water, without much change. B.B. fuses to a semimetallic slag, which is magnetic; with borax and salt of phosphorus a clear bead colored by iron which becomes opaque and whitish on cooling. In acids hardly attacked. Ficinus obtained in his analysis:

| $\overline{\text{P}}$ | $\dddot{\text{S}}$ | $\dot{\text{Fe}}$ | $\dot{\text{Mn}}$ | $\dot{\text{Ca}}$ | $\dddot{\text{Si}}$ | $\dot{\text{H}}$ |
|---|---|---|---|---|---|---|
| 12·82 | 4·07 | 58·85 | 6·82 | 0·17 | 0·17 | 16·87 |

Kenngott remarks that it is probably not vivianite, but more nearly related to the triphyline group.

**Fluolite.**—A mineral of this name from Iceland, mentioned in Glocker's Mineralogy, is a pitchstone, according to Kenngott (Min. Not., No. 12). H.=6·5; G.=2·24. Greenish black in the mass and vitreo-resinous. Composition according to v. Hauer:

| $\dddot{\text{Si}}$ | $\overline{\text{Al}}$ | $\overline{\text{Fe}}$ | $\dot{\text{Mn}}$ | $\dot{\text{Ca}}$ | $\dot{\text{Mg}}$ | $\dot{\text{K}}$ | $\dot{\text{Na}}$ | $\dot{\text{H}}$ (ign.) |
|---|---|---|---|---|---|---|---|---|
| 67·470 | 13·375 | 1·785 | *trace* | 3·025 | *tr* | 1·380 | 2·870 | 9·500 = 99·405 |

The oxygen ratio afforded for $\dot{\text{R}}$, $\overline{\text{R}}$, $\dddot{\text{Si}}$, $\dot{\text{H}}$ is 2·1 : 6 : 34·4 : 8·1.

**Franklinite** [p. 106].—The following important note is by Mr. George J. Brush having been received by letter dated Freiberg, Jan. 27, 1855.

*Note on Abich's analysis of Franklinite.*—In consulting Abich's monograph on the Spinel group,* the writer has observed some errors in the calculations of the analysis of Franklinite† which it may be well to note. In this analysis, Abich obtained 68·88 $\overline{\text{Fe}}$, which, considering the iron to exist in the mineral as magnetite ($\dot{\text{Fe}}\,\overline{\text{Fe}}$), he erroneously makes equivalent to 47·52 $\overline{\text{Fe}}$ and 21·34 $\dot{\text{Fe}}$, the correct numbers being 45·93 $\overline{\text{Fe}}$ and 20·67 $\dot{\text{Fe}}$.

Again, 1·094 grm. $\dot{\text{Mn}}\,\dddot{\text{S}}$ he calculated as equal to 0·440 grm. $\dot{\text{Mn}}$; it should be 0·515 grm. which on 2·690 grm. mineral used for analysis gives 19·14 $\dot{\text{Mn}}$, or 21·29 $\overline{\text{Mn}}$, instead of 16·44 $\dot{\text{Mn}}$ or 18·17 $\overline{\text{Mn}}$, the amount stated by Abich. The analysis corrected reads:

| $\overline{\text{Fe}}$ | $\dot{\text{Fe}}$ | $\overline{\text{Mn}}$ | $\dot{\text{Zn}}$ | $\overline{\text{Al}}$ | $\dddot{\text{Si}}$ | $\dot{\text{Mg}}$ and $\dot{\text{Cd}}$ |
|---|---|---|---|---|---|---|
| 45·93 | 20·67 | 21·29 | 10·81 | 0·74 | 0·40 | *traces* = 99·84. |

(45·93 + 20·67 = $\overline{\text{Fe}}$ 68·88)

* Pogg. Ann., xxiii, 305.

† *Ibid.*, p. 345. The errors do not appear to be typographical.

**Garnet** [p. 196].—Black garnet or melanite occurs with feldspar at Warren, Chester Co., Pa. The aplome of Keim's mine, Pa., is rather a brown garnet than true aplome.

Analysis of the fine red garnet from Yonkers, N. Y., sometimes called pyrope, and also of another similar from Green's Creek, Delaware Co., Pa., by F. A. Genth, Am. J. Sci., [2], xix, 20.

**Galactite.**—Description by Kenngott (Min. Not., No. 11). A zeolitic mineral in needles, which have cleavage parallel to a rhombic prism, near 91° in angle (v. Zepharovich). Color partly reddish white. Lustre of fracture vitreous, H. =4·5–5; G. =2·21. In a tube yields water, and becomes opaque white. B.B. intumesces and fuses easily to a clear colorless glass, and shows a siliceous skeleton on cooling. Gelatinizes readily in heated muriatic acid. Mean of analyses by C. v. Hauer:

| | $\dddot{\text{Si}}$ | $\dddot{\text{Al}}$ | $\dot{\text{Ca}}$ | $\dot{\text{K}}$ | $\dot{\text{Na}}$ | $\dot{\text{H}}$ at ign. | $\dot{\text{H}}$ at 100° C. |
|---|---|---|---|---|---|---|---|
| | 46·99 | 26·84 | 4·36 | 0·45 | 9·68 | 10·56 | 0·49 = 99·37 |
| [Oxygen, | 24·89 | 12·53 | 1·24 | 0·07 | 2·50 | 9·38 | |

The oxygen ratio for the protoxyds, peroxyds, silica and water, as deduced by v. Hauer, is 0·305 : 1 : 2·629 : 0·784, for which von Hauer writes 2 : 6 : 15 : 5, and deduces the formula 2($\dot{\text{Na}}$, $\dot{\text{Ca}}$) $\dddot{\text{Al}}$ + 5$\dot{\text{H}}$ $\dddot{\text{Si}}$. From the Kilpatrick Hills, and Dunbarton, Scotland. [Recalculating the oxygen ratio as given in the second line in the analysis, we obtain 3·81 : 12·53 : 24·89 : 9·38, or nearly (supposing a small deficiency in the protoxyds) 1 : 3 : 6 : 2, the ratio of natrolite; whence galactite is probably *Natrolite*.—D.]

**Geocronite** [p. 85].—Probably occurs at Tinder's Gold mine, Louisa Co., Va., according to Dr. F. A. Genth, Am. J. Sci., [2], xix, 19.

**Gieseckite** [p. 233].—Analyses of gieseckite, from Greenland, by von Hauer (Jahrb. geol. Reichs., 1854, 76, and J. f. pr. Chem., lxviii, 27), with also the analyses of Stromeyer (Gott. gel. Anz., iii, 1993, 1819), and Pfaff (Schw. Jahrb., xlv, 103):

| | $\dddot{\text{Si}}$ | $\dddot{\text{Al}}$ | $\dddot{\text{Fe}}$ | $\dot{\text{Fe}}$ | $\dot{\text{Mn}}$ | $\dot{\text{Mg}}$ | $\dot{\text{K}}$ | $\dot{\text{H}}$ | |
|---|---|---|---|---|---|---|---|---|---|
| 1. Kangerdluarsak, | 46·40 | 26·60 | — | 6·30 | *trace* | 8·35 | 4·84 | 6·76 = 99·36, | *v. Hauer.* |
| 2. " | 45·36 | 27·27 | | | | 7·39 | | 6·87 | *v. Hauer.* |
| 3. Akulliarasiarsuk, | 46·08 | 33·83 | 3·36 | — | $\dddot{\text{M}}$ 1·16 | 1·20 | 6·20 | 4·89 = 96·71, | *Strom.* |
| 4. " | 48·0 | 32·5 | 4·0 | — | —— | 1·5 | 6·5 | 5·5 = 98·0, | *Pfaff.* |

Von Hauer deduces the ratio for the silica, alumina, protoxyds, and water, 4 : 2 : 1 : 1 (or exactly 4 : 2·05 : 0·92 : 1·00, which affords him the formula $\dot{\text{R}}^3$ $\dddot{\text{Si}}$+$\dddot{\text{Al}}^2$ $\dddot{\text{Si}}^3$+3$\dot{\text{H}}$) differing considerably from the other analyses. Stromeyer observes that his material may not have been quite pure from the feldspar with which it was mixed. Haidinger, Tamnau, Blum and Kenngott have taken the ground that gieseckite is altered elæolite or nepheline. The mineral analyzed by von Hauer became brownish red after heating; and it was partly soluble in muriatic acid.

**Gold** [p. 7].—At Beresofski, gold is sometimes interlaced with crystallized galena. (Communicated by G. J. Brush.)

**Gyrolite** [p. 305].—According to L. Sæmann, a specimen of gyrolite examined by him was mixed or interlaminated with another, presenting all the characters of pectolite; and he suggests that pectolite, on losing its alkali, takes a lamellar texture and becomes gyrolite; and losing its lime becomes okenite. (Communicated.)

**Harringtonite** [p. 328].—Analysis of Harringtonite by C. von Hauer (Kenngott's Min. Notiz., No. xi):

| $\dddot{\text{Si}}$ | $\dddot{\text{Al}}$ | $\dot{\text{Ca}}$ | $\dot{\text{Mg}}$ | $\dot{\text{Na}}$ | $\dot{\text{H}}$ at ign. | $\dot{\text{H}}$ at 100° C. |
|---|---|---|---|---|---|---|
| 45·07 | 26·21 | 11·32 | *trace* (?) | 3·75 | 12·93 | 1·41 = 100·69 |

whence the oxygen ratio for $\dot{\text{R}}$, $\dddot{\text{R}}$, $\dddot{\text{Si}}$ and $\dot{\text{H}}$ is 1 : 3 : 6 : 3, and the composition is observed to be that of mesolite.

**Haarcialite.**—This name in Dufrenoy's Mineralogy, arose from a mis-reading of a label of Haarzeolith: L. Sæmann. (Communicated.)

**Helvin** [p. 194].—An analysis of helvin by Rammelsberg (Pogg. Ann., xciii, 455, afforded the following results, to which Gmelin's is subjoined:

| S | $\dddot{\text{Si}}$ | $\dddot{\text{Be}}$ | $\dot{\text{Mn}}$ | $\dot{\text{Fe}}$ | | |
|---|---|---|---|---|---|---|
| 5·71 | 33·13 | 11·46 | 49·12 | 4·00 | = 103·42, | *Ramm.* |
| 5·06 | 33·26 | 12·03 | 40·45 | 5·56 | ign. 1·15 = 97·51, | *Gm.* |

Supposing the 5·71 of sulphur combined with manganese (of which it requires 9·77 p. c., and makes 15·48 sulphuret of manganese), the analysis becomes, according to Rammelsberg:

Mn S 15·48 $\dddot{S}i$ 33·13 $\ddot{\bar{B}}e$ 11·46 $\dot{M}n$ 36·50 $\dot{F}e$ 4·00 = 100·57

giving the formula, Mn S + [($\dot{M}n$, $\dot{F}e$)$^3$ $\dddot{S}i$ + $\ddot{\bar{B}}e$ $\dddot{S}i$], and not according with the garnet formula.

[Although this does not precisely sustain the writer's formula given in his Mineralogy, a comparison of the percentage corresponding to his formula with the above may be of some interest; the percentage is as follows:

Mn S 14·6 $\dddot{S}i$ 34·1 $\ddot{\bar{B}}e$ 9·6 $\dot{M}n$ + $\dot{F}e$ 41·7 = 100.—D.]

Helvin has been obtained at Brevig, Norway, in a zeolitic gangue: L. Sæmann. (Communicated.)

Heteromerite [p. 199.]—In the Jahrb. k. k. geol. Reichsanstalt for 1853, at p. 155, C. v. Hauer published an analysis of heteromerite from Slatoust as given in the Min., p. 169. In Kenngott's Min. Notizen, No. 10, Kenngott publishes a different result by v. Hauer as follows:

| $\dddot{S}i$ | $\ddot{\bar{A}}l$ | $\dot{C}a$ | $\dot{M}g$ | $\dot{F}e$ | ign. |
|---|---|---|---|---|---|
| 36·59 | 22·25 | 34·81 | *trace* | 4·56 | 0·55 = 98·76, |

This analysis gives the oxygen ratio for the protoxyds, peroxyds and silica, 3½ : 3 : 6, which if taken at 3 : 3 : 6=1 : 1 : 2 is the ratio of idocrase, to which species Kenngott refers it, as had been done before the analysis in 1853.

Kenngott in this paper reviews the analyses of idocrase, comparing the proportion of the protoxyds and peroxyds, but not, what is of more importance, the oxygen ratio of all the bases and silica.

Hornblende [p. 170].—*Nordenskiöldite* according to Kenngott (Min. Not., No. 12) is a variety of tremolite occurring mixed with calcite. An analysis by v. Hauer of a specimen containing 38·27 p. c. of carbonates, is given.

Hudsonite [p. 160].—Kenngott observes (Min. Notizen, No. 11) that the Hudsonite has a cleavage parallel to a prism of 124°, like hornblende, and is near hedenbergite, in composition.

[On reëxamining this mineral, which is like sahlite in structure, we find, besides the basal planes of lamination, an orthodiagonal cleavage distinctly inclined about 106° to the base, and also another varying much in angle, but in general making an angle with the diagonal of about 135°; the last appears to correspond to the lateral faces of the prism of pyroxene. No cleavage parallel to a prism of 124° is apparent on our specimens.

The oxygen ratio deduced by Kenngott from his recalculations of the analysis of Brewer, is the same given by the writer, that is 14·91 : 30·42 = 1 : 2 for the oxygen of the protoxyds and $\dddot{S}i$ + $\ddot{\bar{A}}l$.

The recent analysis of Smith and Brush,

| | $\dddot{S}i$ | $\ddot{\bar{A}}l$ | $\dot{F}e$ | $\dot{M}n$ | $\dot{C}a$ | $\dot{M}g$ | $\dot{K}$ | $\dot{N}a$ | ign. |
|---|---|---|---|---|---|---|---|---|---|
| | 38·94 | 10·42 | 30·49 | 0·60 | 10·35 | 3·00 | 2·48 | 1·66 | 1·95 |
| Oxygen, | 20·63 | 4·87 | 6·70 | 0·13 | 2·96 | 1·21 | 0·41 | 0·43 | |

gives for the oxygen ratio for the protoxyds and silica ($\ddot{\bar{A}}l$ included) 11·84 : 25·50, which is intermediate between the hornblende and augite ratios, the former requiring 11·84 : 26·64, the latter 11·84 : 23·68. The mineral analyzed, we have reason to know, had every appearance of purity.—D.]

HYALOPHAN, *von Waltershausen.*—Description and analysis by von Waltershausen (Pogg., xciv, 134). Form monoclinic and resembling orthoclase; *I* : *ii* (see figure 421 of orthoclase, Min., p. 242) =120° 36, *O* : 1*i* =130° 55½′, 1*i* : *I*=111° 55′. By calculation, *C* (or inclination of vertical axis) = 64° 16′ 8″. Color white. H. =6·5; G. =2·711–2·832. Crystals single, or in groups of two or three. Analysis (mean result):

| $\dddot{S}i$ | $\ddot{\bar{A}}l$ | $\dot{C}a$ | $\dot{M}g$ | $\dot{N}a$ | $\dot{B}a$ | $\dddot{S}$ | $\dot{H}$ |
|---|---|---|---|---|---|---|---|
| 24·127 | 49·929 | 1·570 | 0·420 | 5·742 | 14·408 | 2·702 | 0·650 = 99·543 |

giving the formula $3\dot{R}^2\dddot{S}i + 5\ddot{\bar{A}}l^3\dddot{S}i + \dot{B}a\dddot{S}$ = Silica 24·03, alumina 50·52, lime 1·57, magnesia 0·42, soda 5·75, barytes 15·08, sulphuric acid 2·63. Occurs with barytocelestine in the dolomite of the Binnen Valley.

[In this formula, the first member has the oxygen ratio 2 : 3, the second 9 : 3, a very wide diversity. Considering the oxygen ratio of the bases and silica, we observe that this ratio, according to the above, is 24·67 : 12, or nearly 2 : 1, which is the ratio in staurotide, as if the compound might possibly come under the general formula $(\dot{R}^3, \ddot{\bar{R}})\,\dddot{Si}$. It is remarkable that the crystalline form should be almost identical with that of orthoclase, suggesting the idea of a pseudomorph,—against which view however, the hardness of the mineral and its bright faces seem to stand opposed.]

**Iodyrite** or **Iodic Silver** [p. 95, 506].—Analysis of the Chilian iodyrite by Damour (Ann. d. Mines, [5], iv, 329): Iodine 54·03, silver 45·72=99·75, (mean of two analyses) corresponding to Ag I². Specific gravity 5·707 at 8° C. Becomes deep orange at 300° C. but resumes its yellow color on cooling.

**Iridosmine** [p. 19].—Claus found palladium in the iridosmine of the Urals.

**Keilhauite** [p. 341].—Description by D. Forbes (Edinb. N. Ph. J., [2], i, 62). Monoclinic, according to crystals obtained by Mr. Dahl at Arkeroen, Norway. [See angles below]. Some of the crystals weighed 2½ lbs.; the faces were rough and the angles were measured only by the common goniometer. The crystals were generally twins (fig. 2). G. =5·53 at 60° F. Analysis:

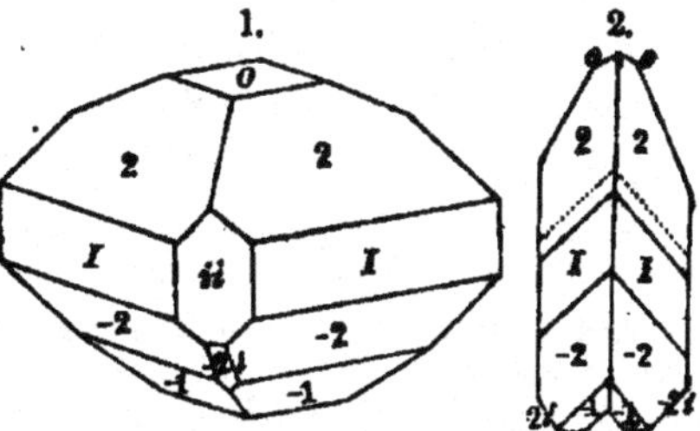


| | $\dddot{Si}$ | $\ddot{Ti}$ | $\bar{\bar{Al}}$ | $\bar{\bar{Be}}$ | $\dot{Ca}$ | $\dot{Y}$ | $\dot{Fe}$ | $\dot{Mn}$ |
|---|---|---|---|---|---|---|---|---|
| | 31·33 | 28·84 | 8·03 | 0·52 | 19·56 | 4·78 | 6·87 | 0 28 = 99·41 |
| Oxygen, | 15·06 | 11·18 | 3·75 | 0·32 | 5·56 | 0·95 | 1·52 | 0·06 |

The analysis agrees nearly with those of Erdmann and Scheerer. Taking the $\ddot{Ti}$ as base, the oxygen ratio of the silica and bases is then 2 : 3, and the formula, Dr. Forbes observes, may be $(\dot{R}^3, \ddot{\bar{R}})\,\dddot{Si}$, which is the same as that of sphene.

[These results afford a complete confirmation of the writer's conclusion respecting the basic relation of the titanic acid in sphene, and also of his published view of Keilhauite. As the above formula for sphene has not been written as above except by the writer recently in this Journal, xviii, 130, and his Mineralogy, Dr. Forbes obviously adopts the view, and agrees with the writer in objecting to the so-called silico-titanates and silico-tantalates. The resemblance in formula between keilhauite and sphene is mentioned in this Journal and in the writer's Mineralogy. This important paper adds the confirmation required by showing that the *form* is monoclinic like sphene: and more than this, what the paper does not recognise, that the angles are closely like those of sphene. The accompanying figure 1 is drawn from the data afforded by the figures; the lettering is like that of sphene in the places referred to. The corresponding lettering of Dr. Forbes and of Brooke and Miller is here given:

| *O* | 2 | *I* | −2 | −1 | *ii* | −2*i* | *Dana.* |
|---|---|---|---|---|---|---|---|
| *a* | −*o* | T | +*o* | *s* | M | *n* | *Forbes.* |
| *y* | *n* | *r* | *t* | *l* | *c* | . | *B. & M.* |

The following are the angles measured by Dr. Forbes; and in a separate column the corresponding angles of sphene are given from Brooke and Miller:

| Keilhauite. | | Sphene, B. and M. | |
|---|---|---|---|
| *I* : *ii* = 147° | - - - - - | (*r* : *c*) | 146° 44′ |
| −2 : −1 = 149° | - - - - - | (*t* : *l*) | 150° 17′ |
| −*ii* : 2*i* = 125° | - - - - - | (*c* : *v*) | 126° 26′ |
| *O* : *ii* = 122° | - - - - - | (*y* : *c*) | 119° 33′ |
| 2 : *I* = 153° 30′ | - - - - - | (*n* : *r*) | 152° 45′ |
| 2 : *O* = 143° 30′ | - - - - - | (*n* : *y*) | 141° 36′ |

From calculations made by Mr. Hansteen, *O* : *I* is given as 114° 25′ 43″; it is 114° 21′ in sphene; *O* : −1 is given at 140° 42′, while it is 139° 20 in sphene.

Considering the roughness of the faces, the approximation is close. The form of the crystal is very near the variety lederite of Shepard. See the writer's Min., ii,

268. The twins resemble those of sphene, being compounded parallel to the plane *ii*. These results therefore confirm entirely the announcement by the writer that keilhauite and sphene are related.—J. D. D.]

LANTHANITE [p. 456].—J. Lawrence Smith, Amer. J. Sci., [2], xviii, 378.

LEUCHTENBERGITE [p. 294].—Observations on the crystallization of leuchtenbergite by Kenngott, Min. Not., No. 12.

MATLOCKITE [p. 127].—Angles according to Kenngott (Min. Not., No. 11), 1 : 1 (basal edge) = 121° 2′; 2*i* : 2*i* (basal edge) = 136° 17′.

MELINITE of unknown locality. Melinite is a hydrous silicate of alumina. Analysis by v. Hauer (Jahrb. Geol. Reichs., 1853, 828):

| $\dddot{Si}$ | $\overline{\overline{Al}}$ (by loss) | $\overline{\overline{Fe}}$ | $\dot{C}a$ | $\dot{H}$ |
|---|---|---|---|---|
| 46·54 | 26·79 | 14·92 | 0·39 | 11·36 (of which 1·08 lost at 100° C.) = 100 |
| 46·47 | 40·82 | | —— | 11·64 " 1·06 " " |

Corresponds to 10·27 silica, 7·08 peroxyds, and 11·42 water.

MICA [p. 225].—M. N. de Kokscharov announces that according to his measurements the mica of Vesuvius is not hexagonal but trimetric with the habit monoclinic.

Note on the optical character of mica, by Grailich, Sitzungsber., Wien, xii, 536.

See further, *Biotite*, *Phlogopite*.

MIMETENE [p. 401].—Mimetene and a *vanadate* of lead occur at the Wheatley Mine, near Phœnixville, Pa.: J. L. Smith, Am. J. Sci., [2], xix, 127.—Analysis of mimetene of Caldbeck Fell, Cumberland, by C. Rammelsberg, (Pogg., xci, 316):

| $\overline{\overline{As}}$ | $\overline{\overline{P}}$ | $\dot{P}b$ | $\dot{C}a$ | Pb | Cl |
|---|---|---|---|---|---|
| 18·47 | 3·34 | 68·89 | 0·50 | 7·04 | 2·41 = 100·64 |

corresponding to $3\dot{P}b^3$ ($\overline{\overline{As}}$, $\overline{\overline{P}}$) + Pb Cl. G. = 7·218. In muriatic acid soluble with difficulty, but perfectly.

MISPICKEL (Arsenikkies) p. [62, 509].—Analysis by *Freitag*, Rammelsberg's Handw. 5th Suppl. 55; by *C. v. Hauer*, Jahrb. k. k. geol. Reichs., iv, 400; *Ragsky*, ib., 328. See also Lieb. u. Kopp Jahresb., 1853, 779.

MOLYBDATE OF IRON.—The occurrence of a mineral containing molybdic acid and sesquioxyd of iron, in Heard Co., Georgia, which is probably a molybdate of iron, is announced by Mr. W. J. Taylor. It is in deep yellow silken tufts, formed of delicate fibres or acicular crystals coating quartz, and resembles the California molybdate described by D. D. Owen.

MOLYBDENITE [p. 66].—Molybdenite occurs in Canada in a vein of quartz intersecting white crystalline limestones north of Balsam Lake, on a small island in Big Mud Turtle Lake. It is associated with greenish scapolite, green cleavable pyroxene and iron pyrites (Logan's Rep. Geol. Canada, 1852–3, 144).

MOSANDRITE [p. 342].—L. Sæmann states in a recent communication to the writer that he has fine specimens of mosandrite in prisms, having the aspect of epidote, thus confirming the suggestions on p. 343 of Min.

NITRE OR NITRATE OF POTASH [p. 433].—Nitre, according to Frankenheim is dimorphous, like carbonate of lime, one form (the common one) prismatic like aragonite, the other rhombohedral like calcite. Both may exist between the temperatures − 10° C. and 300° C. The prismatic ($\alpha$) is normal between these temperatures; the rhombohedral ($\beta$) abnormal, and easily transformed into the prismatic by different influences such as the presence of some foreign substances, or of a crystal of the prismatic kind. At a higher temperature near the fusing temperature of nitre, the rhombohedral is normal and the prismatic abnormal, the latter changing to the former, and retaking again its form as the temperature diminishes.—Pogg. Ann., 1854, xcii, 354.

OLIGOCLASE [p. 239].—Analysis of oligoclase from Zrnin near Krumau in Bohemia, where it occurs in granulite, by v. Hauer (Jahrb. geol. Reichs., 1853, iv, 330):

| $\dddot{Si}$ | $\overline{\overline{Al}}$ | $\dot{C}a$ | $\dot{K}$ | $\dot{N}a$ | $\dot{H}$ |
|---|---|---|---|---|---|
| 68·16 | 23·16 | 3·00 | 0·17 | 9·72 | 0·79 = 100 |

Scheerer presents views in a paper in the Handwört. Chem. of Liebig, Poggendorff, &c., on the composition of oligoclase, and the existence of compounds intermediate between it and orthoclase and albite, one of which he calls oligoclase-albite and the other oligoclase-orthoclase.

ORPIMENT [p. 32.]—Kenngott (Sitzungsber, xi, 982) opposes the view of G. H. O. Volger, that orpiment is in general a result of the alteration of realgar.

OZOCERITE [p. 474].—P. G. Hofstädter in Ann. Ch. u. Pharm., xci, 326, on natural and artificial paraffin.

PALÆO-NATROLITE.—Scheerer, Pogg. Ann., xciii, 95.

PALAGONITE [p. 166].—Observations on palagonite, by Scheerer, Handw. Chem. Lieb., Pogg., &c., 1853.

PARTSCHIN [p. 501].—Description of partschin from Ohlapian, by W. Haidinger (Sitzungsb., xii, 480):—Monoclinic; $C=127° 44'$. Fundamental prism ($\infty$)=91° 52′, a clinodiagonal prism of 116°. The planes without lustre, and measurements only approximations. Cleavage indistinct.

H. =6·5–7. G. =4·006, C. v. Hauer. Lustre weak greasy. Slightly subtranslucent. Composition according to C. v. Hauer:

| | $\dddot{Si}$ | $\dddot{Al}$ | $\dot{Fe}$ | $\dot{Mn}$ | $\dot{Ca}$ | $\dot{H}$ |
|---|---|---|---|---|---|---|
| 1. | 35·28 | 19·03 | 14·38 | 29·11 | 1·82 | 0·38 = 100 |
| 2. | 34·89 | 18·95 | 13·86 | 29·34 | loss 2·77 | |

whence, as v. Hauer observes, it has the garnet oxygen ratio, 1 : 1 : 2, and garnet formula. Haidinger remarks upon the mineral as dimorphous with garnet, and especially with the variety spessartine.

[The oxygen ratio of partschin is the same with that of allanite, which species too, is dimorphons with garnet. Moreover the form also is near that of allanite; and hence it is in all probability a closely related mineral. The angle 127° 44′ corresponds to $O : 1i = 128° 45'$ in allanite: the prism 91° 52′ is the clinodome $\frac{3}{2}i$, which would be 93° 42′ in allanite. The discrepancies in angle are not so large as they appear, when it is noted that the faces are rough.—D.]

PHLOGOPITE [p. 224].—Kenngott endeavors to show in his Min. Not., No. 13, (1) that the mineral called phlogopite by Shepard and Dana is not Breithaupt's phlogopite; and (2) that it is not optically biaxial. On the *first* point he remarks that the description does not agree with Breithaupt's description; *ergo* it cannot be the mineral he described. On the *second*, he states that in his observations with a polariscope, the appearances are the same as for the *biotite* of Greenwood Furnace, and hence the ellipses observed are only distorted circles.

[These are both errors. The specimen of phlogopite on which Breithaupt instituted the species *was sent him by Prof. Shepard*, and Prof. Shepard received soon after a letter mentioning that he had so named it.* Hence Prof. Shepard was not ignorant of the mineral or its locality, nor were other American mineralogists to whom American micas and localities are familiar. When Prof. Shepard stated the angle at 120° to 121° 15, while Breithaupt said 121° 15′, it was because he had found 120° the angle from his many specimens; while irregularities allowed of the

* NOTE BY PROF. SILLIMAN, JR.—As M. Kenngott has suggested a doubt as to the correctness of our recognition of the mica called phlogopite by Breithaupt—inasmuch as he asserts that the characters of the micas described in Shepard's and Dana's works on Mineralogy by that name do not correspond with those given by Breithaupt to the mica from Antwerp, N. Y.,—it is well for me to state in the absence of Prof. Shepard, that our first knowledge in America of Breithaupt's species phlogopite was from a letter written by the Saxon Mineralogist to Prof. Shepard, and which I had the pleasure of reading. In that letter he first applies this name to a reddish yellow somewhat brownish mica from Antwerp, Jefferson Co., N. Y., associated with calcite and serpentine, a specimen of which Prof. Shepard had sent to him not long before. A portion of this same specimen I saw in Prof. Shepard's hands at the time alluded to, and from its entire similarity to other known specimens of the locality and those I have since measured (from one of which the figure beyond has been made) there cannot be the smallest doubt of our correctness. I may add, that all the micas from that portion of Northern New York, which I have seen and examined with reference to their optical characters, belong to the species *phlogopite* with angles from 7° to 17°; or to biotite, and not to muscovite.

variation to 121° 15′. In fact no mica affords normally for the vertical prism (if not oblique) any other angle but 120° and its supplement 60°; this is the angle of the basal cleavage section in all cases. It is useless to consider other characters mentioned by Breithaupt; for Kenngott would have made no such argument if he had been aware of the facts.

The error as to the optical characters arose from the examination of too thin a plate.

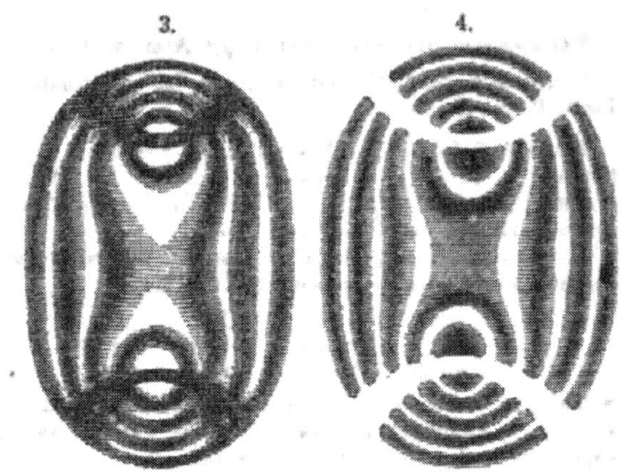


The annexed figures by the writer from a thick plate ($\frac{1}{8}$th of an inch) render words unnecessary. They are from an Antwerp (Natural Bridge) mica, the same in locality with that sent Breithaupt;* and moreover are very similar to the phlogopites of Edwards, Pope's Mills, and other localities, as the writer has especially observed. The figures are made from views just now shown the writer by Prof. Silliman, Jr. The angle between the apparent optical axes has just been measured by Prof. Silliman, and found to be 15° to 15½°. The results of the measurements of different phlogopites are given in the writer's Mineralogy, p. 219.

Whether biotite is a distinct species is another question. The chemical composition of phlogopite, as far as known, is different, the oyygen ratio for $\dot{R}$, $\ddot{\bar{R}}$, $\ddot{S}i$, being 3 : 2 : 5, or perhaps 7 : 4 : 11, while in biotite it is 1 : 1 : 2. But both of these ratios appear to occur in idocrase, while the latter is characteristic of garnet. There is here a subject for further investigation.

It is unnecessary to follow Kenngott in his review of the analyses.—D.]

PICRANALCIME [p. 318].—The crystals of picranalcime, a specimen of which the writer has received from E. Bechi, are as clear and glassy as any analcime and show no evidence of alteration.—D.

PITCHSTONE [p. 248].—The pitchstone of St. Natolia, Sardinia, afforded Delesse Bull. Soc. Geol. de France, xi, 105):

| $\ddot{S}i$ | $\ddot{\bar{A}}l$ | $\dot{F}e$ | $\dot{M}n$ | $\dot{C}a$ | $\dot{M}g$ | $\dot{K}$ | $\dot{N}a$ | H and organic |
|---|---|---|---|---|---|---|---|---|
| 62·59 | 16·59 | 3·17 | 0·55 | 1·16 | 2·26 | 6·48 | 3·14 | 3·90 = 99·83. |

Resembles a black pitch and is associated with trachyte.

A review of analyses of pitchstone is given by Scheerer, Handw. Chem. Lieb., Pogg., &c., 1854. See also *Fluolite.*

PITKARANDITE.—"A paramorphic amphibole species," Scheerer, Pogg. Ann., xciii, 100. Habit that of augite. Color leek-green, light or dark. From Pitkaranda in Finland. Composition according to R. Richter:

| | $\ddot{S}i$ | $\ddot{\bar{A}}l$ | $\dot{F}e$ | $\dot{M}n$ | $\dot{C}a$ | $\dot{M}g$ | $\dot{H}$ |
|---|---|---|---|---|---|---|---|
| | 61·25 | 0·41 | 12·71 | 0·83 | 9·17 | 13·30 | 2·52 = 100·19 |
| Oxygen, | 31·80 | 0·19 | 2·82 | 0·18 | 2·62 | 5·32 | 2·24 |

whence Scheerer deduces the oxygen ratio for the silica and protoxyds, 31·93 : 11·69 = 11 : 4. [Excluding the water the ratio is 31·80 : 10·94 = nearly 12 : 4 = 3 : 1 or taking for the atomic weight of silica 566·25, which is most generally adopted, it becomes 32·45 : 10·94, which is very closely 3 : 1, the ratio of some steatite.—D.]

PLATINA [p. 12].—The name platina is not a diminutive of *Plata, silver*, but signifies *silver-like:* E. Uricochoea of Bogota, Inaug. Dissert.

* Both the Vrooman's Lake and Natural Bridge localities are in Antwerp, and the micas are of similar character, differing a little only in the optical angle. Breithaupt's specimen came from Natural Bridge.—D.

Plumbocalcite [p. 438].—Von Hauer obtained in an analysis of plumbocalcite from Leadhills, Scotland, 92·43 carbonate of lime and 7·74 carbonate of lead = 100·17. G. = 2·772; H. = 3·0. White to pale reddish-white. Kenngott's Min. Not., No. 13.

Polyhalite [p. 377].—H. Rose states (Pogg. Ann., xciii, 1) that according to an examination of the mineral from Vic in Lorraine (that analyzed by Berthier) by Mr. Dexter, the gray variety as well as the red consists of polyhalite, mixed with a hydrous silicate of magnesia and alumina. An analysis of the polyhalite of Hallein by Behnke, and of that of Aussee by Mr. Dexter, afforded:

| | $\dot{Ca}\,\dddot{S}$ | $\dot{Mg}\,\dddot{S}$ | $\dot{K}\,\dddot{S}$ | $\dot{Na}\,\dddot{S}$ | Na Cl | $\dddot{Si}$ | $\dot{H}$ | |
|---|---|---|---|---|---|---|---|---|
| 1. | 42·29 | 18·27 | 27·09 | 2·60 | 1·38 | 0·27 | 6·10 | = 98·00, B. |
| 2. | 45·62 | 18·97 | 28·39 | 0·61 | 0·31 | 0·32 | 6·02 | $\dot{Mg}$ 0·49, $\ddot{\bar{Fe}}$ 0·24 = 100·97, D. |

Analysis 1, contains also 1·35 p. c. of basic sulphate of sesquoxyd of iron.

Prosopite [p. 502].—Scheerer in Poggendorff's Annalen, xcii, 612, has made some additions to his observations on prosopite, but without any complete analysis. A somewhat similar mineral from Schlackenwald is described.

Pyrophyllite [p. 303].—Analysis by Dr. F. A. Genth, of pyrophyllite from Crowder's Mtn., N. Carolina, in Am. J. Sci., [2], xviii, 410. The analyses lead to the formula $\ddot{\bar{Al}}{}^{2}\,\dddot{Si}{}^{5}+2\dot{H}$.

Pyrites [p. 54].—Specific gravity of 52 crystals, according to von Zepharovich, between 3·769 and 5·185, the lowest, of crystals partially altered to limonite: polished crystals 4·8–5·185. Kenngott's Min. Not., No. 11.

PYRORETIN, *Reuss*.—Pyroretin is a new fossil resin from the Brown Coal formation near Aussig in Bohemia, described by A. E. Reuss (Sitzungsb., xii, 551). It occurs in plates sometimes an inch thick and in nodules; is brittle; brownish-black; greasy resinous in lustre; hardness of gypsum; streak-powder dull wood-brown. Burns easily with a reddish yellow flame and a smell like burning amber, leaving a black coaly residue. Heated, it blackens and melts easily, and begins to intumesce from incipient decomposition, and on cooling forms a black asphaltum-like mass. Begins to melt at 100° C., and if kept at this temperature gives off oxygen. Analysis by J. Staněk:

Carbon 80·02 Hydrogen 9·42 Oxygen 10·56

corresponding to the formula $C_{40}H_{28}O_4$. It is near the Beta resin of the Pinus Abies according to Johnson, which gave $C_{40}H_{29}O_5$, differing only by 1 atom of water. Dissolves in hot alcohol, and is deposited again on cooling.

Pyroxene [p. 158].—Analysis of augite from Sasbach, by E. Tobler, (Ann. Ch. u. Pharm., xci, 230):

| | $\dddot{Si}$ | $\ddot{\bar{Al}}$ | $\dot{Fe}$ | $\dot{Mn}$ | $\dot{Ca}$ | $\dot{Mg}$ | $\dot{Na}$ | $\dot{K}$ | $\dot{H}$ | |
|---|---|---|---|---|---|---|---|---|---|---|
| | 44·40 | 7·83 | 11·81 | 0·11 | 22·60 | 10·15 | 2·13 | 0·65 | 1·08 | = 100·72 |
| Oxygen, | 23·52 | 3·65 | 2·62 | 0·02 | 6·46 | 3·92 | 0·55 | 0·11 | 0·91 | |

If the alumina replaces silica, the formula is that of augite, the oxygen ratio being 13·68 : 27·37 = 1 : 2.

Other new analyses, Lieb. u. Kopp. Jahrsb., 1853, 797.

Kenngott has observed the prism $\infty$–$\frac{3}{2}$ in a diopside from Schwarzenstein in the Tyrol. (Min. Not., No. 13.) This mineralogist has reviewed in the same paper the analyses of pyroxene with reference to the alumina.

Pyroxenic Rocks.—A paper on the original composition of some pyroxene rocks, by E. Söchting, is published in the Halle Zeitschr. für die gesammten Naturwissenschaften, Sept., 1854, iv, 194.

Pyrrhotine [p. 50].—The magnetic pyrites of meteoric irons is found by Dr. J. Lawrence Smith to be a protosulphuret of iron, corresponding to the formula Fe S (instead of $Fe^{7}S^{8}$) = Sulphur 36·36, iron 63·64. Analysis afforded Sulphur 35·67, iron 62·38, nickel 0·32, copper *trace*, silica 0·56, lime 0·08 = 98·91. G. = 4·75. Am. J. Sci., [2], xviii, 380.

Retinite, see *Pitchstone*.

Ripidolite, see *Clinochlore*.

Saline efflorescence *from the Desert of Atacama.*—F. Field, Quart. J. Chem. Soc., vii, 308. A few miles to the east of the port of Caldeca in the north of Chili, the soil for many leagues around is white with a saline efflorescence looking like a recent fall of snow. An analysis afforded:

$\dddot{\mathrm{S}}$ 42·60 Cl 19·63 $\dot{\mathrm{Na}}$ 27·17 $\dot{\mathrm{Ca}}$ 6·72 $\dot{\mathrm{Mg}}$ 4·75 $\dot{\mathrm{H}}$ 12·30

with traces of oxyd of iron and carbonates of lime and soda; which corresponds to the following, part of the sodium being united to the chlorine:

$\dot{\mathrm{Na}}\dddot{\mathrm{S}}$ 41·77 $\dot{\mathrm{Ca}}\dddot{\mathrm{S}}$ 16·32 $\dot{\mathrm{Mg}}\dddot{\mathrm{S}}$ 13·75 Na Cl 15·60 $\dot{\mathrm{H}}$ 12·30 = 99·74

It is perfectly soluble in cold water, if added in sufficient quantities and digested with it for a long time. Soluble in dilute hydrochloric acid with scarcely perceptible effervescence. Slightly alkaline to test paper, owing probably to a trace of carbonate of soda. Dissolved in water at 100° F. and allowed to cool, it deposits large crystals of sulphate of soda. One pound of the soil produces more than its own weight of crystallized sulphate of soda.

Scapolite [p. 201].—Analysis of a scapolite from near Perth, Canada, by T. S. Hunt (Logan's Rep. Geol. Surv. Canada, 1852–53, p. 168) found in a boulder; H. =5·5; G. =2·640–2·667; color greenish-gray; subtranslucent:

| $\dddot{\mathrm{Si}}$ | $\bar{\dddot{\mathrm{Al}}}$ | $\dot{\mathrm{Fe}}$ | $\dot{\mathrm{Ca}}$ | $\dot{\mathrm{Mg}}$ | $\dot{\mathrm{K}}$ | $\dot{\mathrm{Na}}$ | ign. |
|---|---|---|---|---|---|---|---|
| 46·30 | 26·20 | 0·60 | 12·88 | 3·63 | 2·88 | 4·30 | 2·80 = 99·59 |

It differs from ordinary scapolite in the large proportion of potash and also the magnesia present.

Scorodite [p. 419, 511].—Occurrence in Cabarras Co., N. C., F. A. Genth, Am. J. Sci., [2], xix, 23.

Scolecite [p. 328]—.Analysis of scolecite from the E. Indies, by W. I. Taylor in the laboratory of Dr. F. A. Genth, Am. J. Sci., [2], xviii, 410.

Seladonite (Terre Verte).—The analysis, p. 511 of Min. is published also in the Ann. d. Mines, [5], iv, 351.

Serpentine [p. 282, 511]—The crystals of serpentine from Easton, Pa., were examined and pronounced pseudomorphs after hornblende and augite by G. Rose (Pogg., lxxxii, 511). The angles of the augite form given by Rose, agree closely with those of augite; one only gave a discrepancy, that of $O:ii$, which was 1° 48′ less. Hermann has since measured the hornblendic form (Pogg., xcii, 287), and finds considerable divergence from unaltered hornblende. He obtained $-1:-1=142°\ 57'$ (instead of 148° 30′), and $O:ii=112°\ 4'$ (instead of 104° 50′). He regards both these hornblendic and augitic forms, as *new species of serpentine* and not pseudomorphs.

[The writer has received a hornblendic serpentine crystal from Dr. E. Swift of Easton, which gives for $-1:-1$, 148° 15′–148° 30′, using the reflecting goniometer (with the reflection of the light of a candle); and approximately 104½–105° for the edge $-1:-1$ on $ii$ (an uneven rounded plane) with the common goniometer; (it is 106° in hornblende). The variations from the hornblende angles are therefore evidently irregularities, and there is no sufficient reason for regarding the crystals as other than pseudomorphs. Dr. Swift observes that there are unaltered crystals of augite and hornblende of similar form in the same vicinity.—d.]

Severite [p. 504].—Analysis of severite from St. Sévère, in France, by C. v. Hauer (Jahrb. geol. Reichs., 1853, 826):

$\dddot{\mathrm{Si}}$ 44·42 $\bar{\dddot{\mathrm{Al}}}$ 36·00 $\dot{\mathrm{Ca}}$ 0·65 $\dot{\mathrm{H}}$ 18·40, (of which 2·95 lost at 100° C.) = 99·47

Corresponds to 9·8 parts of silica, 7 alumina and 17·17 water. Amorphous and earthy, with a white color.

Silver Glance.—The ore of Prince's Location, Lake Superior, is chiefly native silver in thin laminæ in calcite with quartz, silver glance, copper glance, blende and erythrite; some assays of the crude ore afforded T. S. Hunt 8·5 p. c. of silver containing a little gold. (Logan's Report Geol. Surv. Canada). Horn silver is said to have been found there.

Smithsonite [p. 447].—Herrerite of Del Rio has been shown by Dr. F. A. Genth to be a cupriferous Smithsonite. (Proc. Acad. Nat. Sci. Philad., vii, 232).

Spherulite and Retinite or Pitchstone [p. 248].—Analysis by Delesse (Ann. d. Mines [5], 457):

| | $\dddot{\mathrm{Si}}$ | $\bar{\mathrm{Al}}$ | $\dot{\mathrm{Fe}}$ | $\dot{\mathrm{Mn}}$ | $\dot{\mathrm{Mg}}$ | $\dot{\mathrm{Ca}}$ | $\dot{\mathrm{K}}$ | $\dot{\mathrm{Na}}$ | ign. |
|---|---|---|---|---|---|---|---|---|---|
| 1. Spherulite, | 72·20 | 15 65 | 1·64 | 0·50 | 0·62 | 0 98 | 1·71 | 5·52 | 1·12=99·49,G.=2·459 |
| 2. Retinite, | 70·59 | 13·49 | 1·60 | 0·30 | 0·70 | 1·31 | 4·29 | 3·52 | 3·70=99·50,G.=28·36 |

Spherulite includes concretions, often somewhat radiated, in pitchstone. The two analyses here given are from the same mass. The formation of spherulite within the retinite is regarded as an impure crystallization of feldspar.

Spodumene [p. 169].—Specific gravity of variety from Sterling, 3·182: J. L. Smith.

Sulphur [p. 22].—A brownish sulphur of Radoboy in Hungary, owes its color according to Magnus (Pogg. Ann., lxii, 657) to mixture with a bituminous substance impregnating a little earthy material, the whole amount of this material being about 0·2 per cent.

Sylvanite [p. 64].—Kenngott has compared (Sitzungsber. Akad. Wien, xi, 977) all the analyses of sylvanite and shown that the ratio between the tellurium (including the antimony) and the other metals varies between 2·48 : 1 and 3·66 : 1, the mean being about 3 : 1.

Tetradymite [p. 21, 512].—Analyses by Dr. F. A. Genth of tetradymite from Fluvanna Co., Va., Am. J. Sci., [2], xix, 16. The results correspond closely with the formula $Bi\,Te^3$ = Tellurium 48·06, bismuth 51·94.

Tetrahedrite (Gray Copper, or Fahlerz) [p. 82, 512.]—Analysis of the mineral from Eldridge's Gold Mine, Va., and Cabarras Co., N. C., F. A. Genth, Am. J. Sci., [2], xix, 18.

Thuringite [p. 290].—Owenite identical with Thuringite, Dr. F. A. Genth, Amer. J. Sci., [2], xviii, 411.

Tungstates.—Wolfram, Scheelite and probably Tungstate of Copper, [Min., p. 502], in North Carolina, F. A. Genth, Am. J. Sci., [2], xix, 22.

TYRITE, D. Forbes.—Resembles euxenite. Occurs in crystals having a square section, but too irregular and unreflecting for measurement. Cleavage none. H. = 6·5; G. = 5·30 at 60° F. 5·56 of a massive piece. Color and lustre same as in euxenite.

Heated in a glass tube decrepitates strongly, evolves water, and the powder resulting from the decrepitation is of a brilliant yellow color. B.B. with borax forms a glass of a reddish yellow color when warm, but colorless on cooling; with salt of phosphorus, soluble with difficulty, the glass greenish yellow while hot, green when cold. Analysis:

| | $\dddot{\mathrm{Cb}}$ | $\bar{\mathrm{Al}}$ | $\dot{\mathrm{Ca}}$ | $\dot{\mathrm{Y}}$ | $\dot{\mathrm{Ce}}$ | $\dot{\mathrm{U}}$ | $\dot{\mathrm{Fe}}$ | $\dot{\mathrm{H}}$ |
|---|---|---|---|---|---|---|---|---|
| | 44·90 | 5·66 | 0·81 | 29·72 | 5·35 | 3·08 | 6·20 | 4·52 = 100·25 |
| Oxygen, | | 2·64 | 0·23 | | 0·77 | 0·35 | 1·38 | 4·02 |

Taking the atomic weight of tantalum for that of columbium, the oxygen ratio of bases and silica is 5·23 to 11·31, [which is that of Columbite]. Occurs with euxenite at a place called Hampemyr, Norway.

Warwickite [p. 395].—Analysis of warwickite by T. S. Hunt,* (Amer. J. Sci., [2], xi, 352):

$\ddot{\mathrm{Ti}}$ 31·5   $\dot{\mathrm{Mg}}$ 48·5   $\dot{\mathrm{Fe}}$ 8·1   Loss on ignition 2·0 = 85·1

This analysis was made on the small lustrous unchanged crystals. G. = 2·89. The loss in the analysis, which for want of material was not investigated, is explained by the recent discovery of boracic acid by Dr. J. Lawrence Smith.

Specific gravity, according to G. J. Brush, of fresh small crystals of warwickite, 3·351; of large crystals, 3·423. (Communicated.)

On p. 231, Min., vol. i, the proportion of boracic acid in warwickite should be stated at 15 to 20 per cent.

* Mr. Hunt's Enceladite was instituted as a species on the large crystals of the warwickite, which had undergone, as he suggests, partial alteration. The composition obtained differed totally from Prof. Shepard's results (as have all other examinations), and appeared at the time to indicate that the mineral was a distinct species.

WITTICHITE (Kupferwismutherz), [p. 88].—Analyses 1, 2, by R. Schneider (Pogg. Ann., xciii, 305 and 472),—and 3, R. Schenck (Ann. Ch. u. Pharm., xci, 232):

| | | | |
|---|---|---|---|
| Sulphur, | 16·15 | 15·87 | 16·64 |
| Bismuth, | 51·83 | 50·62 | 52·51 |
| Copper, | 31·31 = 99·29 | 33·19 = 99·68 | 30·85=100 |

Schneider deduces the formula $2\text{Cu}\,S + \text{Bi}\,S^3$, Bi standing for the double atom of bismuth; or $[3\text{Cu}\,S + \text{Bi}\,S^3] + x\,\text{Bi}$, supposing it to contain some metallic bismuth. Schenck gives the formula $2\text{Cu}\,S + \text{Bi}\,S^3$ = Sulphur 19·28, bismuth 50·14, copper 30·58. In his analysis, he obtained 2·54 of iron which he excludes as mixed sulphuret of iron.

WOLFRAM [p. 351].—Analysis of a wolfram from Neuhaus Stollberg near Stassburg, by R. Schneider (Pogg., xciii, 474):

$\dddot{W}$ 76·57   $\dot{F}e$ 18·98   $\dot{M}n$ 4·90   $\dot{C}a$ 0·70   $\dot{M}n$ *trace* = 100·95

The protoxyd of iron and manganese are to one another as 4 : 1.

XENOTIME [p. 401].—The xenotime of Georgia contains, according to Dr. J. Lawrence Smith (Am. J. Sci., [2], xviii, 378), Phosphoric acid 32·45, yttria 54·13, oxyd of cerium with a little lanthanum and didymium 11·03, oxyd of iron 2·06, silica 0·89 = 100·56 = $(\dot{Y}, \dot{C}e)^3 \dddot{P}$.

*Errata and Addenda to Mineralogy.*—VOLUME I.—P. 67, l. 14th fr. top, after 1, *add*, "the plane a regular hexagon."—p. 197, after l. 9, *add*, Xenotime, $O : 1 = 138°30'$. —To p. 238, list of papers on slags, *add*, *Rammelsberg* in Pogg., lxiv, 95, and Lehrbuch der Chem. Metallurgie;—*Hausmann*, Beit. zur Kenntniss der Eisenhohofen Schlachen nebst einem geologischen Anhänge, from Studien des Gött. Ver. Bergm. Freunde, and an abstract in Am. J. Sci., [2], xviii, 422.—*J. D. Dana's* criticisms on Hausmann's paper, Am. J. Sci., ibid.;—*C. T. Jackson*, analysis of a slag from Easton, Pa., Proc. Amer. Assoc., iv, 384 (also this Suppl., under CHRYSOLITE).

VOLUME II.—P. 8, anal. 1, for Linarowski, *read* Syranowski.—p. 32, l. 10 and 11 fr. top, for $i\breve{}$ and $2\breve{}$, *read* $i\breve{2}$, $2\breve{2}$; also in part of edition, for 2, *read* $2\breve{2}$.—p. 40, top l., for Jargionite, *read* Targionite; and the corresponding change should be made in the Index.—p. 44, 5 l. from top, before rock, *read* serpentine.—p. 47, over columns of analyses, *add*, S, Cu, Fe.—p. 102, 28 l. fr. top, for specular iron, *read* magnetite.—p. 117, 9 l. fr. top, *trf.* G. =4·56–4·66 to line above after Syenite; and in 8 l. fr. top, after Bay, *dele* and.—p. 130, 6th analysis, for Breithaupt, *read* Brandes; and 7th analysis, for Breithaupt, *read* Plattner, and after $\dddot{S}i$, *add*, and loss—p. 138, l. 12 fr. bottom, *add* $\dot{C}u$ and $\dot{H}$ before 2nd and 3d columns of analysis.—p. 171, in f. 359, 360, for $1i$, *read* $-1$, and for $O, -1i$.—p. 181, 22 l. fr. top, for $\ddot{F}e$, *read* $\dot{F}e$.—p. 189, 19 l. fr. top, transpose 72·85 and 27·15.—p. 190, 6 l. fr. top, for 25·14, *read* 55·14.—p. 204, in analysis 10, the 6·68 is water.—p. 210, 12 l. fr. bottom, *dele* "at St. Paul's, Canada West."—232, l. 18 fr. bottom, for $\frac{4}{3}$, *read* $\frac{3}{2}$.—p. 256 and 257, in formula of Gehlenite, for each $\frac{3}{4}$ and $\frac{1}{4}$, *read* $\frac{1}{3}$.—p. 269, l. 14 fr. bottom, put the semicolon of l. 15th after Island; and in l. 15, for Yemaska, *read* Yamaska.—p. 274, 17 l. fr. bottom, insert after C. W., "with idocrase and garnet" from the next line.—p. 279, before analyses of Crocidolite, *add* Analyses by Stromeyer (Pogg., xxiii, 153).—p. 284, in analysis 26, *add* $\dot{N}a$ 0·90, and in last l., for Westchester, Chester Co., *read* Texas, Lancaster Co.—285 anal. 1 of Metaxite, for $\dot{F}e$, *read* $\ddot{F}e$.—p. 318, anal. 1, for 35·12, *read* 55·12.—p. 360, 21 l. fr. top, for Nischne Tagilsk, *read* Beresofski; and where Beresof occurs, it should be Beresofski.—p. 389, l. 24 from bottom, for $\dot{F}e$, *read* $\ddot{F}e$.—392, 5 l. from bottom, for Danburite, *read* Datholite.—p. 395, l. 19 from top, for $\dot{F}e$ *read* $\ddot{F}e$.—457, 2 l. from top, for Waltershausen, *read* Wachtmeister.—p. 503, l. 20 fr. bottom, for Kenngott, *read* Kokscharov.—p. 505, l. 17 fr. top, for G. A. Brush, *read* G. J. Brush.—Add, aknowledgments to R. P. Greg, Jr., for figures of crystals of Leadhillite, Susannite, Linarite, Triphyline. The author would mention again his obligations to Mr. Greg for various important facts respecting British mineralogy, and also for many communications relating to European minerals and localities, which were most generously contributed.

P. 497, in Canada localities, for Aubert, *read* Aubert-Gallion: after Boucherville *add* Mountain: for Polton *read* Potton; after St. Norbert, for Amethyst, *read* Apatite; after WALLACE MINE, *add* Arsenical and Sulphuret of Nickel, and Nickel Vitriol; after BRUCE'S MINES, another locality, *add* Copper glance, Erubescite: *add* PRINCE'S LOCATION, on Lake Huron (see above, SILVER GLANCE). The author is indebted for the list of Canada localities to Logan's Rep. Geol. Canada, and to Mr. T. S. Hunt.

P. 498.—*On the Geological Ages of the Crystalline Limestones;* (Communicated). —The crystalline limestones of northern New York, and those of the whole of the north side of the St. Lawrence Valley are by Mr. T. S. Hunt referred to the Laurentian [Azoic] System of rocks, which underlies the New York system, while the marbles of western Vermont, of Berkshire Co., Mass., of northwestern and southwestern Connecticut, and of southern New York, N. Jersey and Pennsylvania belong to the Trenton group of Lower Silurian rocks. The serpentines and dolomites which are found all along the eastern line of these limestones from Lower Canada through Vermont and Massachusetts, to Winchester and Litchfield, Conn., and which are again seen at New Haven, Milford and Hoboken, appear to belong to the upper part of the Hudson River group; while the limestones extending from Lake Memphremagog, down the Connecticut River Valley, to Halifax, Vt., and thence through Coleraine, Ashfield, Deerfield, Whately and Bernardstown in Mass., are Upper Silurian; to which also belong the calcareo-micaceous rocks of western Connecticut, and probably those of Bolton farther east in the same State. The limestones of eastern Massachusetts, as in Chelmsford, Bolton and Boxborough, and those of Walpole and Attleborough, he supposes to be of Devonian and Carboniferous age. The same crystalline minerals occur alike in the highly altered rocks of the Laurentian, Lower Silurian and Devonian systems. See Mr. Hunt's paper in the Am. Jour. Sci., [2], xviii, 193.

CPSIA information can be obtained
at www.ICGtesting.com
Printed in the USA
LVOW03s1338250816
501847LV00016B/348/P

9 781278 0263